Modern Rope Seamanship

Synthetic and Natural Fibres

By the same authors:

Deck Seamanship Colin Jarman (Adlard Coles Ltd)
Coastal Cruising Colin Jarman (A & C Black)

Plain Sailing Bill Beavis (Stanley Paul)
A–Z of Cheaper Boating Bill Beavis (Stanley Paul)
Under Way Bill Beavis (Lutterworth Press)
Sailors' Crafts Bill Beavis (George Allen & Unwin Ltd)

Modern Rope Seamanship

Synthetic and Natural Fibres

Colin Jarman and Bill Beavis

ADLARD COLES LIMITED
GRANADA PUBLISHING
London Toronto Sydney New York

Published by Granada Publishing in
Adlard Coles Limited, 1976
Reprinted 1977
Second Edition, 1980

Granada Publishing Limited
Frogmore, St Albans, Herts AL2 2NF
and
3 Upper James Street, London W1R 4BP
Suite 405, 4th Floor, 866 United Nations Plaza,
New York, NY 10017, USA
Q164 Queen Victoria Buildings, Sydney,
NSW 2000, Australia
100 Skyway Avenue, Toronto, Ontario,
Canada M9W 3A6
PO Box 84165, Greenside, 2034
Johannesburg, South Africa
61 Beach Road, Auckland, New Zealand

Copyright © 1976 and 1980 Colin Jarman
and Bill Beavis

ISBN 0 229 11644 2

Printed in Great Britain by
Butler and Tanner Limited,
Frome and London

Granada ®
Granada Publishing ®

Contents

1 Glossary

A *rope* is composed of three *strands* twisted together usually in a right-hand spiral. Occasionally a left-hand *lay* is used, but this is not common. The direction of lay is defined as being *right-hand* when the strands spiral away from you in a clockwise direction, and *left-hand* when they spiral in an anticlockwise direction.

Each strand is itself composed of *yarns* twisted together in the opposite direction to that of the rope's lay. That is to say they are laid up in a left-handed pattern in the strands of a right-hand laid rope.

Finally each of these yarns is made up of *fibres* twisted together in the opposite direction to the lay of the yarns in the strands, i.e. in the same direction as the lay of the rope. Thus it can be seen that the strands, yarns, and fibres are each laid up in a direction opposite to their internal composition. This is done to ensure that the rope binds snugly within itself and tends to stay laid up and not to unravel.

Many ropes are of *plaited* construction, either a solid plait or with a plaited outer skin and a plaited or laid core – a *core and sheath* rope. As with a three-strand rope, the parts of a plaited rope, the strands, are made up of smaller fibres usually running parallel to each other rather than being laid. A plaited rope does not have any inherent twist or lay. Figure 1.1 shows the construction of a variety of ropes: plaited

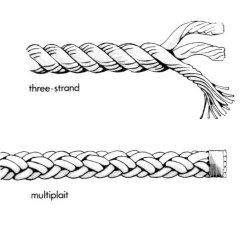

three-strand

multiplait

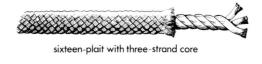

sixteen-plait with three-strand core

braided with braided core

Fig. 1.1 The four principal types of rope

core and sheath; three-strand, right-hand laid rope; multiplait; plaited sheath and laid core.

Throughout all ropework there are certain basic terms used to denote the various parts of a rope in which a knot is being formed. These are shown in fig. 1.2 where

1

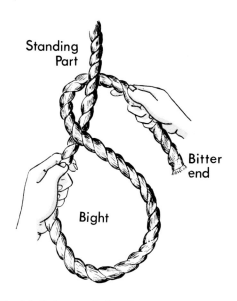

Standing
Part

Bitter
end

Bight

Fig. 1.2 Basic terms for knot forming

Fig. 1.3 Turn

Fig. 1.4 Round turn

the *standing part* is coming from a fixed point and the *working part* (the part being used to form the knot) has been looped back on itself to form a *bight*. Above this bight a *turn* has been taken around the standing part, and the right hand is holding the *bitter end*.

Figures 1.3 and 1.4 illustrate the difference between a turn and a *round turn*. In the former the plaited rope passes round the three-strand rope in a single bight coming back on itself in a 180-degree turn, while in the round turn, the plaited rope goes right round and back on itself in a 540-degree turn.

A large part of this book is devoted to variants of three basic things, namely knots, bends, and hitches. A *knot* is some combination of loops, mostly interlocking, used to fasten ropes together or to objects, or to enlarge the end of a rope. A *bend* is a knot used in the joining of two ropes, or the securing of a rope to an eye, ring, becket, spar, etc., which may be cast off easily when required. A *hitch* is a knot whose constituent loops jam together in use, particularly under strain, yet remain easily separable when the strain is removed. A *gantline* is a line rove through a block fixed aloft and is used for hoisting anything (sails, washing, bosun's chairs, etc.).

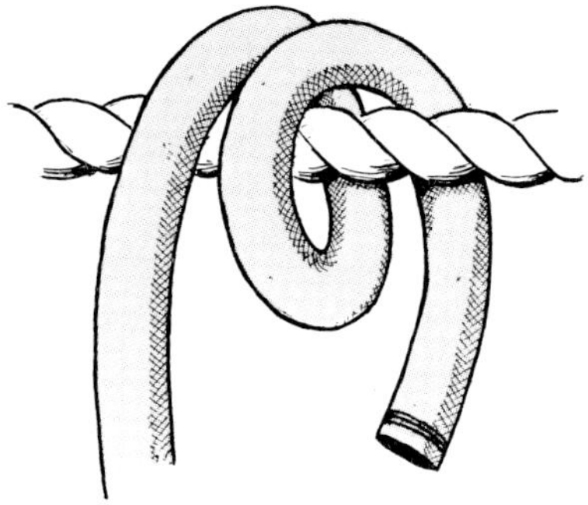

If you think these definitions are a bit woolly, you're absolutely right, but you should find that in practice things are not so bad. In any case it is rarely necessary to trot out such definitions, the ability to form the requisite knot, bend, or hitch being sufficient.

2 Knots for everyday use

Overhand or thumb knot

This is probably the simplest of all knots and forms the basis of several, including the reef knot (page 3). It is used as a temporary stopper knot in light line to prevent it passing through an eye or sheave (though a figure-of-eight (page 4) is more seaman-like for this), and again temporarily to stop the ends of a line fraying.

A bight is formed with the working part, and the end is passed round the back of the standing part before being brought over the top and down through the bight. Figure 2.1 shows the loose knot before it is worked up tight, and fig. 2.2 shows the knot from the other side.

Reef knot

As its name implies, one of the many uses of the reef knot is in tying off the ends of reef points when shortening sail. It can be formed when there is a load on both standing parts, and it can also be untied when under tension by pulling on one end and capsizing the knot. When being used to bend two ropes together care should be taken to ensure compatibility of material and size, otherwise the knot will slip. In fact it is not advisable to use it for this purpose at all.

Fig. 2.1 Overhand knot – loose

Fig. 2.2 Overhand knot – from other side

The reef knot consists simply of two overhand knots, one on top of the other, with the second being formed in the opposite direction to the first (fig. 2.3). This results in the two ends lying back alongside, and on the same side of, their respective

3

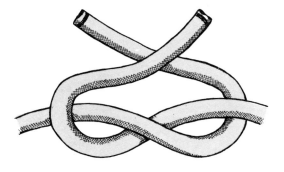

Fig. 2.3 Reef knot (1)

Fig. 2.5 Reef knot in use (1)

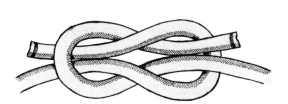

Fig. 2.4 Reef knot (2)

Fig. 2.6 Reef knot in use (2)

standing parts (fig. 2.4), and the whole knot looks neat and symmetrical.

Figures 2.5 and 2.6 show reef knots in use first for securing an anchor in its deck chocks, and secondly for fastening a gasket which has been passed round a furled sail.

Fig. 2.7 Slipped reef knot

Slipped reef knot

When a reef knot that may have to be undone in a hurry is being tied, it is convenient to slip one end (fig. 2.7) so that it can be released simply by pulling that end. It is formed in the same way as a reef knot and should lie in a similarly symmetrical shape. In effect it is like half of the bow used to tie shoelaces.

Figure-of-eight

The figure-of-eight is a stopper knot used in preference to the overhand knot as it is bulkier, and will therefore prevent the end of a line passing through a larger eye; it does not bind so tightly, making it easier to undo when the time comes. It is generally thought of as being the seaman's stopper knot, and is used for example in the falls of halyards and the tail ends of sheets (fig. 2.8).

4

Fig. 2.8 Figure-of-eight – in use

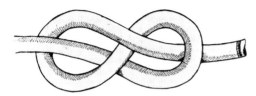

Fig. 2.9 Figure-of-eight – forming (1)

Fig. 2.10 Figure-of-eight – forming (2)

To form a figure-of-eight the working part is laid across the standing part, passed round behind it, and the bitter end is tucked down through the bight (fig. 2.9). The knot may then be worked tight, or left slightly loose as in fig. 2.10 since it will tighten in use (fig. 2.8).

It may be noticed that the knots in figs 2.9 and 2.10 are formed in opposite directions: this is just to show that they may be tied equally well either way.

Bowline

Undoubtedly one of the most useful knots aboard any vessel, the bowline is used to form a standing loop in the end of a line. It is easy to tie and is strong, yet it does not jam impossibly under load.

The first stage of tying a bowline is something of a knack which may need some practice, but once mastered will never fail to produce the correctly formed knot. Hold the standing part of the line in the left hand (fig. 2.11), and taking the bitter end in the

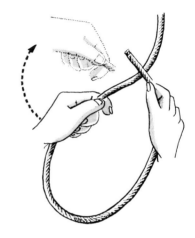

Fig. 2.11 Bowline – forming (1)

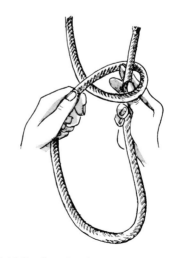

Fig. 2.12 Bowline – forming (2)

right hand, lay it on top of the standing part. Lift the left hand so that the standing part begins to loop over the bitter end which is, simultaneously, being pressed down and in towards the bottom of the large bight. As the standing part loops over it, the bitter end is turned upwards so that it pokes up through the loop (fig. 2.12). The end is then passed round behind the standing part and back down through the loop to finish as in fig. 2.13. The knot is worked tight and you have a bowline. It is shown in fig. 2.14 where it is being used to secure a guy to the end of a boom.

Just occasionally you see someone pass the bitter end round the standing part so that it lies outside instead of inside the main loop of the bowline. This is just as good, but has no advantage.

If the bowline is to stand for some time, or is being formed in a particularly slippery synthetic rope, then it is advisable to seize the bitter end to the side of the loop to prevent it from slipping.

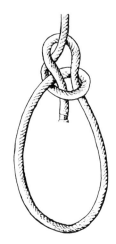

Fig. 2.13 Bowline – forming (3)

Round turn and two half hitches

A round turn and two half hitches is used on many occasions when a line with some load on it is to be secured to a spar of some sort or an eye. Once the full round turn has been taken, the load can be held while the two half hitches are put on for security. It can also be cast off while under tension. Perhaps the most common uses are in securing a dinghy to a mooring ring, or tying fenders to cabintop grabrails. This is the example shown in fig. 2.15.

A round turn is taken on the rail with the working part of the line which is then brought up and over the standing part before being passed back between itself and the round turns. This means that it has been used to take a turn on the standing part and so form the first half hitch. The second half hitch is formed in the same way by rolling

Fig. 2.14 Bowline – in use

the working part on over the standing part and tucking the end back through beside the first hitch. These two half hitches are always formed in the same direction so that

Fig. 2.15 Round turn and two half hitches

Fig. 2.17 Fisherman's bend – in use

Fig. 2.16 Fisherman's bend – forming

they result in a clove hitch (see page 8) around the standing part of the line.

Fisherman's bend or anchor bend

The fisherman's bend is a variation of the round turn and two half hitches and is the only knot to use when bending a warp to an anchor. It is very strong, it holds excellently, and can be undone easily as it does not jam.

The first stage of the fisherman's bend is a round turn on the anchor ring. The end of the warp is then passed round behind the standing part and tucked under the round turn (fig. 2.16). This part is now worked tight as it is the 'holding' part of the bend.

Fig. 2.18 Anchor bend – alternative method

A half hitch is then taken round the standing part and the bitter end is seized to it for security when the anchor is in use. The end result is seen in fig. 2.17.

In fig. 2.18 we see an alternative way of finishing off the anchor bend: that is by tying a bowline with the bitter end on the standing part. This method is used when no seizing stuff is handy and is very strong and reliable.

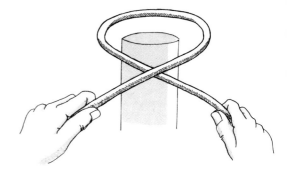

Fig. 2.19 Clove hitch – forming (1)

Clove hitch

The clove hitch is used to secure a line to a fixed object when there will be load applied on both sides of the knot, such as in the case of ratlines or emergency lifelines or guardrails. It should not be used when load will only be applied to one side as the knot will then slip badly.

Initially a turn is taken on the object to which the line is to be secured, with the end passing under the standing part (fig. 2.19). A half hitch is then put on above this turn by passing the end round behind the post or other object, and tucking back under itself in front of the post (fig. 2.20). The knot is worked tight to result in fig. 2.21.

Figures 2.22–2.26 show this process in more detail using the method of dropping loops over the exposed end of a bollard. Where this cannot be done, for example when hitching a line to a stanchion to form a second guardrail, the working part must make the turn and half hitch by being passed around the stanchion and under itself in sequence as described above.

Two uses of the clove hitch are shown in figs 2.27 and 2.28. The first shows two clove hitches one above the other used to attach a burgee halyard to the burgee stick so that, when hoisted, it lies flat against the mast allowing the burgee to fly clear of the truck. Fig. 2.28 shows a line clove hitched round a tiller to hold it central when the boat is at anchor.

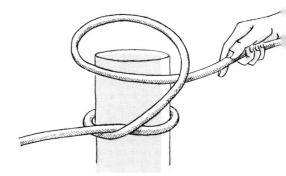

Fig. 2.20 Clove hitch – forming (2)

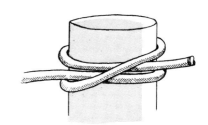

Fig. 2.21 Clove hitch – forming (3)

Fig. 2.22 Clove hitch – over bollard (1)

8

Fig. 2.23 Clove hitch – over bollard (2)

Fig. 2.24 Clove hitch – over bollard (3)

Fig. 2.25 Clove hitch – over bollard (4)

Fig. 2.26 Clove hitch – over bollard (5)

Fig. 2.27 Clove hitch – in use (1)

Fig. 2.28 Clove hitch – in use (2)

Sheet bend or becket bend

The sheet bend is commonly used to join two ropes of differing diameters, as it is not prone to capsizing when a snatch load is applied to one side only. For this reason it is probably better to use the sheet bend for joining two ropes and to reserve the reef knot, which might be thought of as an alternative, for joining the ends of a single line, e.g. the ends of a tier passed around a bundle of sail.

9

Fig. 2.29 Sheet bend

Fig. 2.31 Double sheet bend

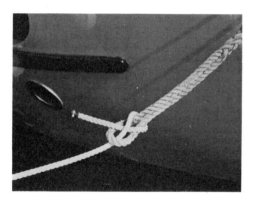

Fig. 2.30 Becket bend

Fig. 2.32 Double becket bend

The bend is formed by passing the end of one line through a bight of the other, then taking a turn around the neck of the bight and tucking under itself (fig. 2.29). Care should be taken to ensure that both the ends of line protrude on the same side of the knot. The sheet bend can of course be tied in the same way as a bowline, using the technique described for that knot on page 5 to form a loop with the end of one line already through it.

The alternative name of becket bend is applied when the same knot is used to attach one line to an eye spliced in the end of another rope. This is shown in fig. 2.30 which also serves to show the opposite side of the bend to that shown in fig. 2.29.

Double sheet bend or double becket bend

The double sheet bend is a more secure way of joining two ropes than the single sheet bend, and is therefore preferred when one of the ropes is at all slippery. It differs from the ordinary sheet bend only by having a full round turn about the neck of the bight (made in the larger rope) before the end is tucked. The completed bend is shown in fig. 2.31, and the double becket bend is shown in fig. 2.32. Again, as with the single sheet bend, care should be taken to ensure that both rope ends emerge from the double sheet bend on the same side.

10

Rolling hitch – formed about a second rope

A rolling hitch is used to attach one line to another when the load on one is to be parallel (or nearly so) to that on the other. It can be used for instance when relieving the load on a line that has become trapped or whose securing point needs to be transferred while strain is maintained on the line.

To form the hitch a turn is first taken as in fig. 2.33, followed by a second made ahead of the first as shown in fig. 2.34. Finally a third turn is rolled on in the same direction, and the end is tucked under itself to keep it secure (fig. 2.35). The load must be applied in the direction of the arrow, to ensure that the load part binds the two turns under itself, thus holding the hitch tight and stopping it from slipping. Chances of slipping are also lessened if the hitch is rolled on in the direction of the rope's lay, as shown in the diagrams. Figure 2.36 shows a rolling hitch in use.

Fig. 2.33 Rolling hitch – forming (1)

Fig. 2.34 Rolling hitch – forming (2)

Rolling hitch – formed about a spar

When hitching a line to a spar instead of to another rope, a slightly different form of the rolling hitch is used. In this case the second turn is not put on ahead of the first, but behind it. The third is still put on ahead. The method of hitching to a spar is shown in figs 2.37 and 2.38, where the back and front of the hitch can be seen.

Fig. 2.35 Rolling hitch – forming (3)

Figure-of-eight loop

While the bowline will be employed on practically every occasion that a loop is required to be formed in the end of a rope, it may not be entirely satisfactory when the rope is of a very slippery synthetic fibre. In this case the figure-of-eight loop can be used.

Fig. 2.36 Rolling hitch – in use

11

Fig. 2.37 Rolling hitch – about a spar (1)

Fig. 2.38 Rolling hitch – about a spar (2)

Fig. 2.39 Figure-of-eight loop – forming

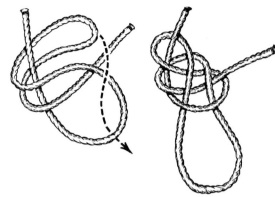

Fig. 2.40 Figure-of-eight loop – on the bight (1)
Fig. 2.41 Figure-of-eight loop – on the bight (2)

Fig. 2.42 Figure-of-eight loop – completion

When it is to be tied through a ring or eye, or around an object that a loop cannot be slipped over, the method of tying shown in fig. 2.39 is used. Here a normal figure-of-eight is tied some way back from the bitter end which is then passed through the ring, becket or whatever, and back up through the lower bight of the figure-of-eight. It is then passed round behind the standing part of the line and brought forward to cross over the front of the figure-of-eight under itself and the other part of the required loop.

On the other hand, when the final loop can be dropped over a bollard, pile or whatever, the figure-of-eight loop is formed 'on the bight'. This method is shown in figs 2.40 and 2.41. Here a large loop is made in the end of the rope and is used to tie a figure-of-eight in exactly the way described on page 4 for the figure-of-eight knot. The end result is shown in fig. 2.42.

3 Knots for special occasions

Cow hitch or lark's head

The cow hitch is usually made by accident when trying to tie a round turn and two half hitches (see page 6). The round turn and first half hitch come out all right, but then instead of making the second half hitch in the same direction as the first, it is made in the opposite direction. The result is a round turn and a cow hitch. However, when formed intentionally the cow hitch is used to secure a line to a ring or spar when strain will come on both ends of the line on the same side of the ring or spar. This may happen for instance when attaching guys to the cringles in an awning. (When strain is put on both ends of the line on *opposite* sides of the strong point a clove hitch is normally used.)

A cow hitch may be formed in two ways. In the first method a turn is taken round the ring (or spar) and the end is passed over the standing part. Then a second turn is taken in the opposite direction to the first, and the end is tucked under itself to form the second standing part. The result is shown in fig. 3.1. In the second method, the rope is centred and the bight passed through the ring (or round the spar), and the two ends are tucked through it. The result is again shown in fig. 3.1. This method is much easier if it can be used.

Figure 3.2 shows the cow hitch being

Fig. 3.1 Cow hitch – forming

Fig. 3.2 Cow hitch – in use

13

used to keep a sail tier ready to hand on a coachroof grabrail. This is quite common practice.

Cow hitch and toggle

The cow hitch (or lark's head) and toggle is a straightforward variation of the cow hitch (page 13) used when the two ends of the line are fixed and only the bight can be passed through the ring. It is perfectly secure while there is tension on both parts of the rope, and it can be released instantly by removing the toggle.

To form the hitch a bight of rope is passed through the ring or round a spar, and a rod such as a marlinspike is inserted under the standing parts and over the bight (see fig. 3.3).

In some cases a toggle can be used in conjunction with the loop of a mooring line when the latter is being secured to a quay-side ring.

Fig. 3.3 Cow hitch and toggle

Constrictor knot

This is a useful knot for securing the neck of a bag or acting as a temporary whipping or seizing. It was developed by Clifford W. Ashley, author of *The Ashley Book of Knots*, and is similar in formation to a clove hitch, but has the property of getting ever tighter as load is applied to its ends and of retaining that tightness when the loads are removed. Thus it will hold securely and may well need some coaxing to undo.

To tie the knot around, say, the neck of a bag, a round turn is taken with the line so that its second half crosses down over the first and the working end returns to the front below the lazy end (fig. 3.4). The working end is then passed upward over the lazy end (lying under the bight of the round turn), and tucked down under it in the form of an overhand knot. At this point the knot is loosely formed and should appear as in fig. 3.5. Once this stage is reached, all that remains to do is tighten the knot to the desired tension (fig. 3.6).

Certainly in the case of tying the neck of a bag, and in any other case where the knot will have to be tied and untied frequently, it is advisable to slip the end in the fashion shown for the slipped reef knot (page 4). This will ensure that the constrictor can be released without difficulty.

Surgeon's knot

Many of today's synthetic fibre ropes and lines, particularly cords and other small stuff, are very slippery and it is not unknown for conventional knots to work loose under stress. One such knot is the reef knot which often does not hold too securely in stiff or slippery lines. If this is likely to be the case, then it is better to use the surgeon's knot instead of a reef knot, since this (as its name implies) has been developed for tying off the perfectly smooth sutures used in operations; and if it holds in that stuff it should hold in most materials.

The formation of the surgeon's knot is very similar indeed to the reef knot; in fact it simply has an extra tuck on each side. An

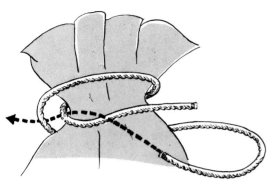

Fig. 3.4 Constrictor – forming (1)

Fig. 3.7 Surgeon's knot

Fig. 3.5 Constrictor – forming (2)

Fig. 3.8 Carrick bend – forming (1)

Carrick bend

The carrick bend is not a well-known knot although it is very useful, being strong, secure and readily undone. It will also happily join two ropes of differing size and material, and is particularly useful for bending on an extra length to an anchor warp. The main drawback to the carrick bend is that it is rather bulky and would not easily pass through a fairlead.

Fig. 3.6 Constrictor – forming (3)

overhand knot is formed and one end is given another turn round the other before the two ends are used again to form another overhand knot (in the opposite direction) and an extra tuck. It can be followed easily in fig. 3.7.

The bend is perfectly symmetrical, and its form can readily be checked as each part passes regularly over and under its neighbour. A loop is taken in one rope, its end passing across beneath its standing part. The end of the other rope is passed

15

Fig. 3.9 Carrick bend – forming (2)

Fig. 3.10 Carrick bend – forming (3)

Fig. 3.11 Carrick bend – completion

across and underneath this loop (fig. 3.8). It is then brought up over the first rope's standing part, down under its bitter end, over one side of the loop, under its own standing part, and finally over the second side of the loop (fig. 3.9). Thus it has been woven alternately over and under each succeeding part. This stage is also shown in fig. 3.10 where an extra line is being attached to a kedge warp. Figure 3.11 shows the finished bend. Here it has been drawn tight resulting in its capsize and the bringing together of the two ends from their previously opposite positions.

In really heavy ropes or particularly stiff ones where the bend will not naturally capsize, the two ends can either be seized or half hitched back onto their standing parts.

When the carrick bend has been in use for some time and has settled, it may be necessary to use a marlinspike to separate the two loops. Normally they will just slide apart.

Fig. 3.12 Waggoner's hitch – forming (1)

Waggoner's hitch or lorry driver's hitch

This hitch obviously does not have its origins at sea; however it is most useful on boats since it provides a 2 : 1 purchase, which is sufficient to bowse down most lashings pretty hard.

The end of the line being used as the lashing is first passed through a ringbolt or round some other strong point. Two bights are formed in the part of the line above the strong point, one downward and one upward (see fig. 3.12). The upward bight is then used in exactly the same way as the end of a rope is used to form a bowline (see page 5). The result should look like the first stage of a bowline and appear as in fig. 3.13. Next the bitter end is brought up and passed through the downward loop as in fig. 3.14. This end is then hauled down to tighten the lashing as required. Figure 3.15 shows a waggoner's hitch in use.

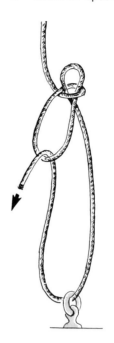

Fig. 3.14 Waggoner's hitch – forming (3)

Fig. 3.13 Waggoner's hitch – forming (2)

Fig. 3.15 Waggoner's hitch – in use

Catspaw

The catspaw is ideally suited to hitching a sling to a hook, as it won't jam and holds best when there is equal strain on both its parts.

A bight of the sling is folded downward over the standing parts as in fig. 3.16, and the two loops so formed are twisted once or twice *outwards* using the standing parts. The hook is then slipped into the bights as in fig. 3.17.

Fig. 3.16 Catspaw (1)

Fig. 3.17 Catspaw (2)

Timber hitch

Not used very often for its true purpose of securing a rope to a log or spar (or number of logs or spars) that is to be towed or lifted, the timber hitch is nonetheless useful since it can be tied quickly and there is no possibility of its jamming. It is often used to fasten the end of a long sail tier (see page 20).

To make the timber hitch an end of rope is passed round the spar (or timber) and then round its own standing part. The end is then dogged (twisted) back down its length as in fig. 3.18. It is not important here where a plaited line has been used, but in the case of a laid rope the dogging must be done in the direction of the lay.

Finally, if the timber hitch is being used for towing, it helps to keep the spar or whatever in line with the tow if a half hitch is tied round it a short way from the timber hitch. This can be seen in fig. 3.19 where two pieces of timber are being lifted from the water.

Fig. 3.18 Timber hitch – forming

Sheepshank

Though seldom used, a sheepshank is a very simple way of shortening a line temporarily, particularly if it is necessary to bypass an area of chafe such as where a boom guy has been sawing against a guardrail.

Assuming that this is the purpose for which you wish to tie the sheepshank, a bight is formed in the line well to one side of the chafed area and is brought back to the standing part on the other side of the chafe. Here it is applied to the standing part in the same way as the bight used in the waggoner's hitch (page 17). The bight left on the opposite side of the chafe is then applied to the standing part on that side in the same way. You should then have a sheepshank as shown in fig. 3.20, where the knot has had one bight stopped to the standing part. This would be done to both bights if the sheepshank were to be in use for any length of time, for instance when it is being used to shorten a mooring line as in fig. 3.21. The stopping is put on to prevent the sheepshank falling apart when the load is eased on the two standing parts, which it will otherwise do.

One useful facet of the sheepshank is that the area of chafe bypassed by it lies on the section of line between the two loops, and it is quite safe to cut this part completely without the knot coming apart – provided tension is retained on both standing parts. Thus a splice can be put in with the whole rope still in use.

Fig. 3.19 Timber hitch – in use

Fig. 3.21 Sheepshank – in use

Fig. 3.20 Sheepshank

Fig. 3.22 Marling hitch

Marling hitch

The marling hitch, or rather a series of marling hitches, is used to bend a sail to its spars (gaff and boom), or for lashing a furled headsail to a guardrail to keep it off the foredeck, or a mainsail to its boom to keep it stowed neatly.

The end of the marling line may be secured with a timber hitch (see page 18) and then, working towards yourself, the line is passed down around the sail, up over the part lying along the sail, and is tucked under itself in a direction on along the bundled sail. This should be made clear by looking at fig. 3.22. To check that the hitch is correctly formed, imagine removing the sail from within the hitch: you should be left with a series of connected overhand knots.

Buntline fisherman's bend

This bend is an amalgamation of a buntline hitch and a fisherman's bend, and was first described by John Mellor in an article published by *Yachting Monthly* magazine in 1974. It is used to secure particularly slippery ropes to anchor rings, bollards, spars, or anywhere that a fisherman's bend would otherwise be used.

The first part is exactly as described for a fisherman's bend (page 7), a round turn being taken on the ring, bollard or whatever, and the working end being passed across the front and tucked back between the turns and the object. It is then passed round the standing part, across itself *towards* the ring, a second turn is taken round the standing part in the same direction as the first and the end is tucked up between the turns to form a clove hitch (previously described on page 8). The result should be as shown in fig. 3.23, from which stage the turns are all worked tight.

An alternative to the buntline fisherman's bend worth mentioning here is the one shown in fig. 3.24, where an ordinary fisherman's bend has been tied and the bitter end has been tucked back into the rope's lay. This is very effective with soft, slippery ropes as a load on the standing part tends to close the lay, thus trapping the end more tightly.

Fig. 3.23 Buntline fisherman's bend

Spar hitch

The spar hitch is similar to a clove hitch and a constrictor knot. It is more secure than a clove hitch when there is a greater load on one end of the rope than the other, and grips better on a smooth spar, but is more easily undone than a constrictor.

To tie the spar hitch, a turn is taken round the spar and the end is passed over the standing part and round the spar again in the same direction. It is then crossed back over the standing part and is tucked under the rope where it first crossed the spar. Figure 3.25 shows this situation.

Sliding figures-of-eight

This bend performs the same function as a carrick bend in joining two similar or dissimilar lines securely, and yet being easily undone.

The bend consists of two figures-of-eight, one in the end of each rope, the other rope being contained in each figure-of-eight's lower loop. Figure 3.26 makes this clear. Once the situation shown in this diagram has been reached, all that remains is to tighten the two knots within themselves, and apply tension to the two standing parts to slide the figures-of-eight together.

When the bend is to be undone, the process is reversed by prising the two figures-of-eight apart. A marlinspike may be needed for this.

Fig. 3.25 Spar hitch

Fig. 3.24 Buntline fisherman's bend – alternative

Fig. 3.26 (*below*) Sliding figures-of-eight

4   Knots for emergencies

Stopper knot

Occasionally it is necessary to relieve the load on one line with another, so that a snarl-up in the first can be cleared or it can be shifted to another cleat or winch. There are several ways of bending one rope to another for this purpose, but the two commonest are a rolling hitch (shown on page 11) and the stopper knot described here. However, the stopper knot has an advantage over the rolling hitch by virtue of being quick to undo – in fact it simply falls apart when the load is removed – and speed is often an essential part of the operation.

As with the rolling hitch, the final pull on a stopper knot must be parallel or nearly parallel to the line under original strain. Following the sequence shown in figs 4.1–4.4, the line to be bent on is turned round the rope under load as in fig. 4.1. It is then crossed on over itself and dogged round the rope under load in the direction of the lay (fig. 4.2). When several turns have been taken, either the end is held by hand or is stopped to the other rope for a more permanent set-up. The load can then begin to be taken by the new line as in fig. 4.3, until finally the load is completely transferred as in fig. 4.4.

It is worth mentioning that the stopper knot can be used with equal success on rope, line, chain (fig. 4.5) or even wire, where a

Fig. 4.1 Stopper knot – in use (1)

rolling hitch would have to be made over a serving of adhesive tape. Incidentally, for extra grip on particularly hard and shiny ropes the end of a rolling hitch can be backed round the rope against the lay and then stopped to it.

Bowline on the bight

Though not very commonly used, a bowline on the bight can form an adequate

Fig. 4.2 Stopper knot – in use (2)

Fig. 4.4 Stopper knot – in use (4)

Fig. 4.3 Stopper knot – in use (3)

Fig. 4.5 Stopper knot – in use (5)

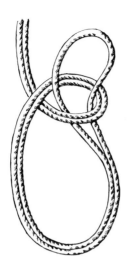

Fig. 4.6 Bowline on the bight – forming (1)

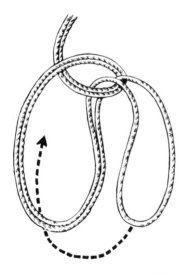

Fig. 4.7 Bowline on the bight – forming (2)

Fig. 4.8 Bowline on the bight – completion

To form a bowline on the bight for use as a bosun's chair, it is first necessary to tie an ordinary bowline (page 5) whose loop is twice the length of those to be formed by the bowline on the bight. This loop then becomes the working end used to tie the bowline on the bight. It is applied to the double standing part (below the first bowline knot) in the usual fashion for starting a bowline (fig. 4.6). The working bight is then opened out and passed up over the double loop (fig. 4.7). It is taken all the way up to the standing part and worked tight as in fig. 4.8. The result is obviously very similar in appearance to a straightforward bowline, but doubled.

Where both ends of rope are fixed and a loop is needed in the middle, then the same process is followed, but of course the initial single bowline is not tied. Care must be taken to keep approximately equal loads on the two ends or else the knot will capsize.

Spanish bowline

The Spanish bowline is another knot producing two loops, enabling it to be used either as a substitute bosun's chair, or for

alternative to a bosun's chair in an emergency, since its two loops are more comfortable to sit in than the single one of an ordinary bowline. However, make no mistake, a proper bosun's chair is far more comfortable! A bowline on the bight is also a simple way of forming a strong loop in the middle of a line whose ends are both fixed or otherwise unavailable.

24

slinging a ladder over the side to act as a paint staging. Its formation is unlike any of the other bowlines and exactly why it gained that name is unknown.

First the rope is centred and laid out in three loops as shown in fig. 4.9. The large loop is then folded downward to lie across the other two loops and the two standing parts, as in fig. 4.10. From there the two outer bights of this large loop are passed outward over the two small loops and brought up through them, following the dotted lines in fig. 4.11. They are pulled well through and adjusted to the required length, and the whole knot is then worked tight as in fig. 4.12.

It will be noticed that the side of the two loops nearer to the standing parts can run through the knot. This means that it is not impossible for the loops to slip, and therefore the Spanish bowline should always be used cautiously.

Fig. 4.11 Spanish bowline – forming (3)

Fig. 4.12 Spanish bowline – completion

Fig. 4.9 Spanish bowline – forming (1)

Fig. 4.10 Spanish bowline – forming (2)

Fig. 4.13 Running bowline

Running bowline

The running bowline is a simple running knot or noose formed by tying a bowline

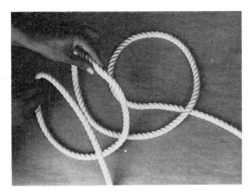

Fig. 4.14 Jury knot – forming (1)

Fig. 4.16 Jury knot – forming (3)

Fig. 4.15 Jury knot – forming (2)

Fig. 4.17 Jury knot – forming (4)

(page 5) round the standing part of the rope in the way shown in fig. 4.13.

Jury or masthead knot

In the unhappy event of finding yourself dismasted at sea you are faced with the problem of setting up a jury mast. The most useful knot for this purpose is the jury or masthead knot, both of which names describe its function, since it is placed at the masthead to form the band to which the stays and shrouds of the jury mast are secured.

First three loops of rope are laid down, one on top of the other, as shown in fig. 4.14. Next they are arranged so that the left-hand part of the bottom loop lies on top of the right-hand part of the top loop, and both are in the centre of the middle loop. This

Fig. 4.18 Jury knot – forming (5)

situation is shown in fig. 4.15. Now pass your hands over and under the outer loops to pick up these two bights, as is being done in fig. 4.16. These two bights are then pulled outward so that they weave over and under the other loops in the fashion shown in fig. 4.17. Once they are pulled out, the

Fig. 4.19 Jury knot – in use

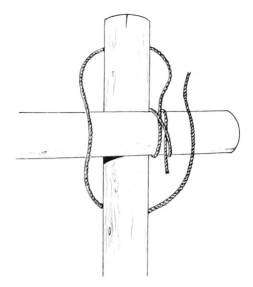

Fig. 4.20 Square lashing – forming

loop lying at the top is pulled upward to form the 'clover leaf' shape in fig. 4.18, and there you have three loops to attach shrouds and forestay to, with space for the mast in the dead centre of the knot. For the back-stay, the two loose ends are tied together with a bowline by applying the short end to the long one which will actually form the stay.

The final figure 4.19 shows the completed set-up at the head of a jury mast with two shrouds, forestay and backstay all secured, the shrouds and forestay being attached by sheet bends. Should it be needed, the jury knot can also be used (in exactly the same way) to secure the heel of the jury mast.

Square lashing

A square lashing is used to hold two spars crossed at right angles. It is begun by form-ing a clove hitch (page 8) around one spar with the end of the line being used for the lashing (fig. 4.20). The working part of the line is then taken back around the other spar, brought forward and down across the first spar, before being passed back around

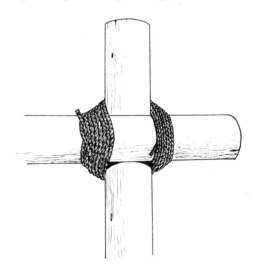

Fig. 4.21 Square lashing – completion

the second spar to emerge at the front by the clove hitch (fig. 4.20). Thus the first round of the lashing is completed. This pat-tern is then repeated several times, each part being hove taut successively, until the two spars are held tightly and securely together. Finally the end is half hitched around one spar to neaten off as in fig. 4.21 which shows the finished lashing.

27

5   Whippings

The main practical justification for using a whipping on synthetic rope is that it can be put on in any weather – try fusing the ends with a match in a gale or a rain storm and you'll soon understand. It is also quite possible for fused ends to be crushed (by clumsy feet for instance) and so unlay, and for them to jam in the swallow of a block. On natural fibre lines however there is no substitute for the old-fashioned whipping and certainly, on any rope, nothing looks better.

Principally, a whipping is used to prevent the rope from unlaying and destroying itself; in fact its name is said to originate from its use to stop reef points from unlaying as they 'whipped' in the wind. It also serves to bind the yarns together tightly so that the end of the line can be passed through a block, fairlead, or eye.

Whippings should be worked towards the end of the rope, with the excess being trimmed off to neaten it when the whipping is finished. The turns are always put on against the lay. As a rough guide the length of the whipping should be equal to the diameter of the rope, while ropes facing particularly hard usage often have a second whipping about one diameter back down the rope from the first. Whippings are generally made with *waxed* synthetic twine to stop them slipping.

Common whipping

Simple and easily remembered, the common whipping is adequate for most jobs, except for lines such as reef points which are liable to flog, throwing the whippings off as they do so. Begin by laying the end of the whipping twine along the rope and then pass the turns tightly over it (figs 5.1 and

Fig. 5.1 Common whipping – forming (1)

Fig. 5.2 Common whipping – forming (2)

Fig. 5.3 Common whipping – forming (3)

Fig. 5.5 Common whipping – forming (5)

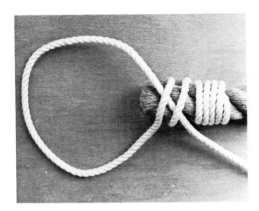

Fig. 5.4 Common whipping – forming (4)

Fig. 5.6 Common whipping – completion (1)

Fig. 5.7 Common whipping – completion (2)

5.2). In this way the end is anchored beneath the turns. The last few turns, however, are left loose so that the working end of the twine may be passed underneath them (figs 5.3 and 5.4). These last turns are then worked tight (fig. 5.5), and the end is drawn down and finally cut off to produce the completed whipping shown in figs 5.6 and 5.7.

Some people like to finish with an overhand knot to stop the end pulling through, but it looks a little unsightly and isn't really necessary. An alternative is to let the bitter end protrude and tie it to the working end in the middle of the whipping, but this too is unnecessary.

A third alternative is to make the bitter end into a long loop that will project beyond the turns when they are laid over it. The turns are then put on and the working end is tucked through the projecting loop and pulled down to the middle of the whipping in a bight. Both ends are then cut off short. This method works well (though it can be hard to pull the ends into the middle if the turns are really tight), but is not a lot simpler than the basic method.

West Country whipping

This is a particularly good whipping to use with synthetic fibre whipping twine as each turn can be held secure. A length of the twine is middled and an overhand knot is formed around the rope's end as shown in fig. 5.8. Another overhand knot is then formed opposite this one at the back of the rope (fig. 5.9). A third knot is tied at the front just above the first, a fourth at the back above the second, and so on, with knots being formed at back and front alternately. This is continued, working towards the end of the rope, until sufficient length has been covered, as in fig. 5.10. The ends of twine are then finished off with a reef knot.

When using particularly slippery synthetic whipping twine it is useful to coat it with beeswax. When forming a West Country whipping it helps to keep the knots secure if a second tuck is put in each overhand knot as though starting a surgeon's knot (page 14), and to finish off with a completed surgeon's knot rather than a reef knot.

Needle-and-palm whipping

As the name suggests, this whipping is made with the aid of a palm and needle. The palm is a leather guard worn around the hand with which to push the needle through a sail, or in this case the rope. The whipping is stitched to the rope so that even if it parts or frays it will not undo completely. It is a neat and permanent whipping, probably the most secure of all.

Use a doubled length of sail twine or whipping twine if that will go through the eye of the needle, and start by taking a couple of stitches through the rope to anchor the end. Pass the turns around the rope in the usual fashion, making sure that they are drawn up tightly. When sufficient

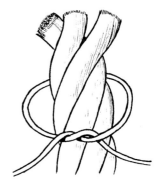

Fig. 5.8 West Country whipping – forming (1)

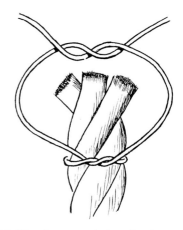

Fig. 5.9 West Country whipping – forming (2)

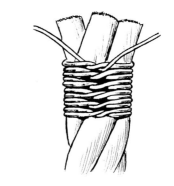

Fig. 5.10 West Country whipping – completion

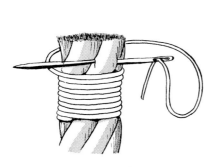

Fig. 5.11 Needle-and-palm whipping – forming (1)

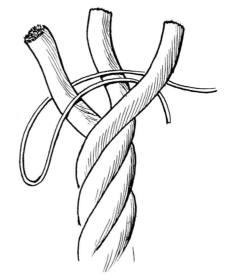

Fig. 5.14 Sailmaker's whipping – forming (1)

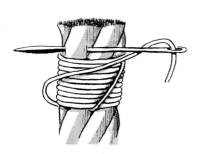

Fig. 5.12 Needle-and-palm whipping – forming (2)

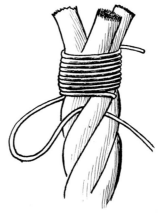

Fig. 5.15 Sailmaker's whipping – forming (2)

Fig. 5.13 Needle-and-palm whipping – completion

Fig. 5.16 Sailmaker's whipping – completion

Fig. 5.17 Alternatives to whipping (1)

Fig. 5.19 Alternatives to whipping (3)

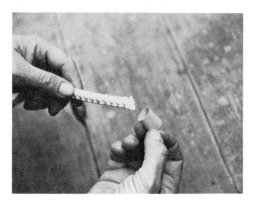

Fig. 5.18 Alternatives to whipping (2)

Fig. 5.20 Alternatives to whipping (4)

turns have been laid on pass the needle through a strand at the top of the rope (fig. 5.11) and worm the twine back over the turns (so that it lies in the spiral groove formed by the strands of the rope). Stitch the twine into the rope through the next strand at the bottom of the whipping and worm the twine up to the top again. Then push the needle behind the next (third) strand at the top (fig. 5.12) and worm the twine down again, repeating this process of stitching and worming from top to bottom until all the spiral turns are doubled. To finish, take a few more stitches through the rope to secure the end of the twine (fig. 5.13). Some people prefer to finish by taking a couple of half hitches round a spiral turn and pushing the knot well down into the lay of the rope.

Sailmaker's whipping

The sailmaker's whipping produces almost exactly the same result as a needle-and-palm whipping without the use of these tools. It is perhaps not quite as secure in that it is not stitched onto the rope, but the difference is marginal.

A loop of whipping twine is laid round one strand of the unlaid end of a rope, with both ends emerging between the other two strands. This starting position is shown in fig. 5.14. The strands are then laid up together and the working end of the twine is used to make the required number of frapping turns about the rope towards its end (fig. 5.15). The original loop of twine is then dropped over the end of the strand it was formed round, and is pulled down

32

tight by pulling on the end projecting from the lay beneath the whipping. This end is wormed up to the top of the whipping and is tied with the end of twine that was used to form the whipping. This process is shown in fig. 5.16 where everything has been left loose for clarity.

When laying up a rope's end as at the beginning of this whipping, the strands can be made to lie together better if they are twisted in the direction of their own lay as they are laid together.

Alternatives to whipping rope's ends

An 'instant' alternative to a proper whipping is to bind the fraying end of a rope with adhesive tape as in fig. 5.17. This is surprisingly effective, but must not be thought of as anything more than a stop-gap measure.

A modern idea is to shrink plastic sleeves onto the rope's end. This method is shown in figs 5.18 and 5.19, where the sleeve, rather larger than the diameter of the rope, is placed over the rope's end and then heated with a match flame. Care must be taken that this heating is only allowed to shrink the sleeve and not to melt it. Once the sleeve has been shrunk completely it grips the rope tightly and is an effective 'whipping'. Removal has to be carried out with a knife.

Finally, the commonest method of dealing with the end of synthetic rope is by sealing it with a match flame. Here the strands of the rope are simply fused together by the flame's heat (fig. 5.20). Achieving a neat end can be tricky, but is helped by binding the end with paper, cutting through that with a sharp knife, and then sealing the end (still bound in the paper to hold it together) before it can unlay. The alternative to this is to melt the ends, wet your fingers and roll the ends together, but *be careful*, else the molten strands will blister your fingertips badly as they stick to the skin.

6   Splicing

Short splice

This is the strongest way of joining two lines together permanently, or of rejoining the ends of a parted rope, but it increases the diameter substantially, making it unlikely to render through a block or eye.

To begin the splice, unlay both rope's ends and put a constrictor knot (page 14) on the end of each strand to stop it fraying. Marry the strands of each rope as in fig. 6.1, and temporarily stop one set of strands to the other rope as shown on the left of fig. 6.2. Then take any one of the free strands and tuck it against the lay, over one strand and under the next of the opposite rope (see fig. 6.2). Tuck the two remaining free strands in the same manner, always over one strand and under the next to look like fig. 6.3. Now remove the stopping and tuck the other set of strands into the first rope in exactly the same way, over one strand and under the next, working against the lay. If the rope is very stiff or tightly laid, it may be easier to open up the strands with the help of a marlinspike or grooved splicing tool.

To finish the splice, tuck each strand on each side once or twice more, over one strand and under the next, against the lay. Then cut the strands off, not too close to the splice or else they will untuck, and roll the splice firmly underfoot to help it settle. The

Fig. 6.1 Short splice – forming (1)

Fig. 6.2 Short splice – forming (2)

Fig. 6.3 Short splice – forming (3)

34

Fig. 6.4 Short splice – completion

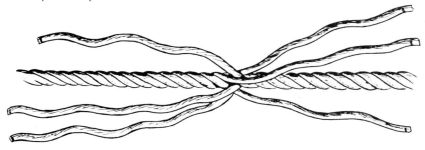

Fig. 6.5 Long splice – forming (1)

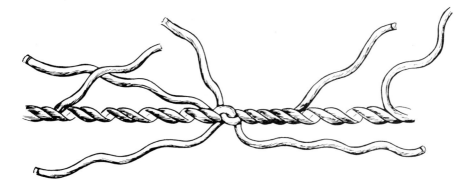

Fig. 6.6 Long splice – forming (2)

Fig. 6.7 Long splice – completion

result should be like fig. 6.4. In this case the ends have been made tiddly by putting a short whipping on, but this is for show and is rarely done in practice. Sometimes however, each emerging strand is halved and seized to its neighbour so making it impossible to pull out.

Long splice

The advantage of a long splice is that it does not appreciably increase the rope's diameter if made properly, thus allowing a line to render through blocks or eyes. The drawbacks are that it takes more rope, is a little

35

weaker than a short splice, and it is decidedly more fiddly to make. Let's say here also that there are many ways of making a long splice and we are just describing one method. Indeed 'different ships, different long splices' is a well-used expression at sea.

First the strands of each rope are unlaid for a considerable distance (about 10 turns) and are married together as in fig. 6.5. One strand on each side is then unlaid for a further distance (about 6 turns) and its opposite number from the other rope is laid in its place. This is done by unlaying one turn and laying the other strand in its place immediately afterwards, turn for turn. The operation is shown in fig. 6.6 where the strands have been unlaid further than recommended for clarity. In practice you should do the right-hand side first, and then do those on the left-hand side. Remember to check at the centre of the splice to ensure that the turns are in their respective places, or in other words that the splice appears as a continuous piece of rope. This is essential and if it is not so, go back and start again.

There should be three pairs of strands along the rope and each of these is now knotted together with an overhand knot as shown in the centre of fig. 6.6. The ends are then cut to equal length (fig. 6.7) and each is halved, by reducing the number of yarns, and is tucked against the lay as shown on the right of fig. 6.7.

Three-strand eye splice

An eye splice is the way to form a permanent loop in the end of a rope and is used more often than any other type of splice.

The strands of the rope are unlaid a short way and the ends are whipped, sealed, or a constrictor knot is applied to stop them fraying. The middle strand is tucked under one strand of the standing part against the lay, at a point to give the required size of loop (fig. 6.8). Take the strand lying on the inside and tuck that under the next strand of the standing part at the same point along the rope (fig. 6.9); don't move any further along the rope. Now turn the work over and tuck the third strand under the remaining strand of the standing part at the same level as the first two strands were tucked. Make sure that this third strand is also tucked against the lay although it will have to double back on itself to do so (fig. 6.10).

Fig. 6.8 Eye splice – forming (1)   Fig. 6.9 Eye splice – forming (2)   Fig. 6.10 Eye splice – forming (3)

Tuck each strand at least three times, over one strand and under the next, working always against the lay. The ends are cut off, but not too short or else they will untuck themselves. The splice is rolled underfoot to help it settle. The result should be as in fig. 6.11.

If so desired the strands can be halved before the last tuck to taper the splice, or they can be divided in two after the last tuck, and each part seized to its neighbour across the intervening strand of the standing part.

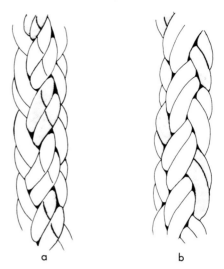

Fig. 6.12 Multiplait eye splice (1)

(Marlow Multiplait has the black marker thread running through the right-handed strands.) In fig. 6.12a, the right-handed strand is shaded; in fig. 6.12b the left-handed strand is shaded.

Form the eye to the right of the standing part and pass two right-handed strands under the convenient right-handed strands on the standing part (fig. 6.13).

Fig. 6.11 Eye splice – completion

Multiplait Eye Splice

The eye splice is based upon the construction of the rope which employs both left-handed and right-handed strands (fig. 6.12). There are two pairs of each which comprise double strands. It is important to identify the left- and right-handed parts.

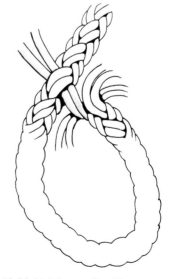

Fig. 6.13 Multiplait eye splice (2)

37

Fig. 6.14 Multiplait eye splice (3)

Fig. 6.16 Multiplait eye splice (5)

Pass the adjacent left-handed strands under adjacent left-handed strands on standing part (fig. 6.14).

Turn the splice over completely and repeat the process, i.e. tuck remaining right-handed strands and left-handed strands under their respective parts on the standing part (fig. 6.15).

Fig. 6.17 Multiplait eye splice (6)

Separate the strands and tuck individually, taking great care not to 'cross over' but keep to the original set of strands (figs. 6.16 and 6.17).

Make five tucks altogether and finish by whipping each strand to its neighbour. Heat seal the ends. Completed splice should have the distinct 'parallel' appearance (fig. 6.18).

Fig. 6.15 Multiplait eye splice (4)

38

Fig. 6.18 Multiplait eye splice (7)

Stitch and whip method of making an eye in plaited rope

The stitch and whip method has been developed as an alternative to splicing. It hasn't quite the same strength as a splice, but it is perfectly satisfactory for sheets, etc., providing care is taken to get the turns good and tight. It is suitable for both eight- and sixteen-plait rope.

Begin by bending the rope to form an eye; the length of the tail measured from the throat of the thimble should be 3 in (75 mm). Thread a suitable-sized sail needle with about ten feet of thick whipping twine and pass the needle as close to the throat of the thimble as you can get it. (You may either use a sailmaker's palm to push the needle through, or it can be pulled through with a pair of pliers.) Leave a long end of thread for this will be used for the whipping (fig. 6.19).

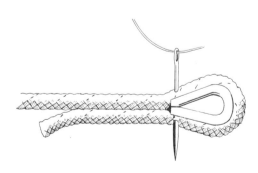

Fig. 6.19 Stitch and whip eye (1)

Stitch the two parts of rope together as shown in the drawing with a double sequence working down to the end of the rope and then back again. The needle should be entered close to the exit of the previous stitch and at a slight angle (fig. 6.20).

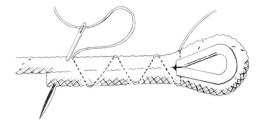

Fig. 6.20 Stitch and whip eye (2)

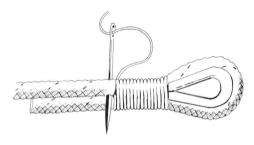

Fig. 6.21 Stitch and whip eye (3)

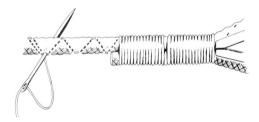

Fig. 6.22 Stitch and whip eye (4)

Cut off short end of twine. Hammer the two parts of rope together, particularly at the throat of the thimble. This will ensure the rope is drawn tight around the thimble and will make it generally more receptive to whipping. Begin the whipping as close to the thimble as is possible and after each few turns, pause to hammer the whipping still closer towards the thimble. When half the

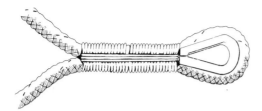

Fig. 6.23 Stitch and whip eye (5)

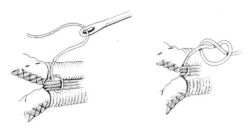

Fig. 6.24 Stitch and whip eye (6)

whipping is complete, put a 'locking' stitch through the standing part of the rope. This effectively separates the whipping so that, should one part break, the remaining half will not be affected (fig. 6.21).

Continue whipping and ensure the twine is kept absolutely tight, hammering up occasionally. Anchor the end of the twine with six stitches through the standing part of rope spread over a distance of about 2 in (50 mm). Cut off surplus twine and the eye is now complete (fig. 6.22).

The Stitch and Whip can also be used as a seizing when an eye is required in the centre of a rope as, for example, in jib sheets. The method is exactly the same except that there is not the same necessity to get the whipping tight into the thimble, because room will have to be left for the 'frapping' turns. There should be two frapping turns in eight-plait rope and three frapping turns in sixteen-plait (easily recognised by having a much smaller and tighter plait). The Stitch and Whip when used as a seizing need only be 2 in (50 mm) long and requires no mid stitch (fig. 6.23).

There are many popular ways to secure the end of the twine, but the easiest method is to stitch a half-stitch: an overhand knot will prevent the end pulling through (fig. 6.24).

Marlow eight-plait eye splice for dinghies only

Suitable for 9 mm and 10 mm diameter sizes. On smaller sizes a stitch and whip is recommended.

Make a loop knot 6 ft (1.8 m) from the end. This will prevent the outer plait being disturbed beyond the area where the splice is to be made (fig. 6.25).

Fig. 6.25 Eight-plait eye splice – dinghies only (1)

Fig. 6.26 Eight-plait eye splice – dinghies only (2)

Slide the outer plait back to expose the inner core. Cut off 27 in (675 mm) from the inner core (fig. 6.26).

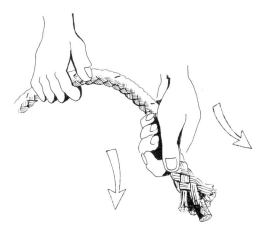

Fig. 6.27 Eight-plait eye splice – dinghies only (3)

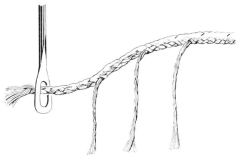

Fig. 6.29 Eight-plait eye splice – dinghies only (5)

Fig. 6.28 Eight-plait eye splice – dinghies only (4)

Fig. 6.30 Eight-plait eye splice – dinghies only (6)

Slide the outer sheath over the core and on to its full extent; this will leave a 'coreless' length equal to 27 in (675 mm). *Make sure all the outer cover is worked back.* (fig. 6.27).

Insert the splicing tool in a position ½ in (12 mm) from the end of the inner core. It should re-emerge 11 in (275 mm) away down the length of the 'coreless' plait (fig. 6.28).

Taper the end of the outer plait to fit through the eye of the splicing tool. This is done by cutting out one yarn 3 in (75 mm) from the end, another yarn 2 in (50 mm) from the end, and a final yarn 1 in (25 mm) from the end. It should now be possible to thread the end of the tapered plait through the eye (fig. 6.29).

Pull out the splicing tool and the tapered end will follow, filling the hollow core, and the splice is now completed. Make sure all the wrinkles in the outer plait are smoothed out and give the rope a snatch to bed the splice down before cutting off the surplus (fig. 6.30).

(Note – since the core is cut out, the strength of the rope is considerably reduced, but it is easily strong enough for dinghy sheets.)

Eye splice for Marlow sixteen-plait sheath and laid core

Unlay the first 6 in (150 mm) of the outer cover. This will expose the three-stranded inner core (fig. 6.31).

Make a knot 8 feet (2.4 metres) from the end of the rope. This is a temporary measure to prevent the lay of the rope being

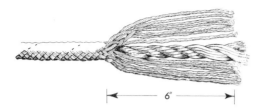

Fig. 6.31 Eye splice – sixteen-plait sheath and laid core (1)

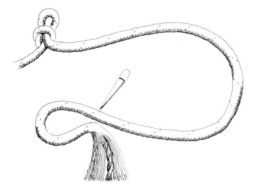

Fig. 6.32 Eye splice – sixteen-plait sheath and laid core (2)

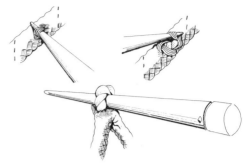

Fig. 6.33 Eye splice – sixteen-plait sheath and laid core (3)

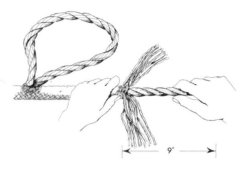

Fig. 6.34 Eye splice – sixteen-plait sheath and laid core (4)

disturbed beyond the area of the splice while in the making (later you will need a strong anchoring point upon which to hook this knot). Form the size of eye required and using a hand spike (Swedish fid is best) make a hole in the outer cover so that a loop of the inner core can be extracted (fig. 6.32).

During this operation it is important not to disturb the outer plait more than necessary. Therefore enlarge the hole carefully as fig. 6.33 shows by first inserting the point of the spike and gently lifting up a group of four yarns.

Continue to lift the groups of yarns which surround the hole until they have been stretched sufficiently and the inner core can be clearly seen.

Bend the rope sharply at this point and it should then be possible to lift out the inner core with the hand spike.

Pull out sufficient of the inner core to make a 6 in (150 mm) eye. Next slide back the outer plait at the end of the rope until 9 in (225 mm) of the inner core is uncovered; in other words you increase this length by 3 in (75 mm) (fig. 6.34).

Splice the end into the loop as you would with an ordinary three-stranded rope splice. Begin the splice 2 in (50 mm) from where the core protrudes: make three full tucks and two tapered tucks (fig. 6.35).

Cut off the ends leaving $\frac{1}{2}$ in (12 mm) tails and bind these very tightly to the body of the rope with tape. Next hook the temporary knot to some secure position and holding the splice in the right hand pull the loose plait over the completed splice until every part of the inner core is drawn inside the body of the rope. It may be necessary to work the loose plait down towards the splice from as far back as the temporary knot (fig. 6.36).

42

Fig. 6.35 Eye splice – sixteen-plait sheath and laid core (5)

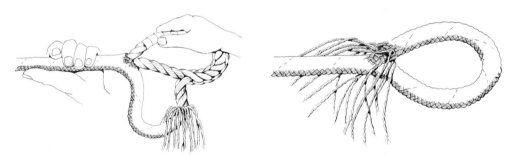

Fig. 6.36 Eye splice – sixteen-plait sheath and laid core (6)

Fig. 6.37 Eye splice – sixteen-plait sheath and laid core (7)

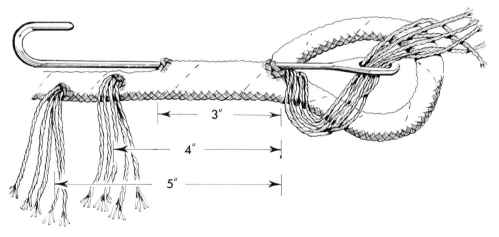

Fig. 6.38 Eye splice – sixteen-plait sheath and laid core (8)

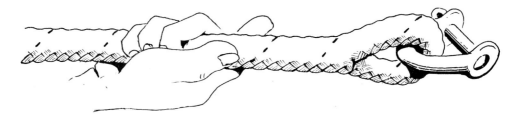

Fig. 6.39 Eye splice – sixteen-plait sheath and laid core (9)

The first part of the splice is now complete and the yarns of the outer plait are ready to tuck (fig. 6.37).

For this operation a splicing needle is used. Push the eye of the needle into the plait at a position 5 in (125 mm) from the throat of the eye and continue to push the needle until it emerges at the throat. Be careful not to snag the rope during this process; the needle should pass between the outer plait and the inner core. Divide the yarns into groups of three and thread the first group into the needle. Withdraw the needle and this will pull the yarns down the length of the rope. Repeat the sequence for the remaining two groups of yarns but each time inserting the needle 1 in (25 mm) nearer the eye (fig. 6.38).

To complete the splice cut off the yarns close to the rope, smooth back the loose plait and these ends will disappear. Finally give the splice a good snatch to bed it down. It is now ready for use (fig. 6.39).

Braidline eye splice

The core-and-sheath Braidline rope requires a unique form of eye-splicing which is considerably more complicated to describe than it is to do. Tools required are a sharp knife, some adhesive tape, a Marina Braidline splicing fid and pusher, and a felt-tip pen.

First step is to bind the end of the rope lightly with a turn of adhesive tape. Measure one fid length back along the rope from this end and make a mark with the felt-tip pen. We will call this point R, and it can be seen in fig. 6.40.

A loop is now formed equal in size to the required eye with R at its throat, and a second mark is made opposite to R : this is called point X and is also shown in fig. 6.40. Measure off a further five fid lengths from X and form a slip knot which can be secured about a fixed object such as a cleat.

Point X is the place from which the core of the rope is extracted. Bend the rope sharply at this point, open the braiding of

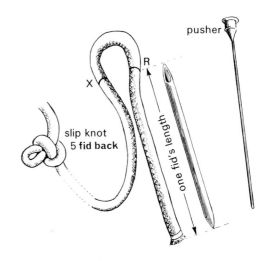

Fig. 6.40 Braidline eye splice – preparation (1)

44

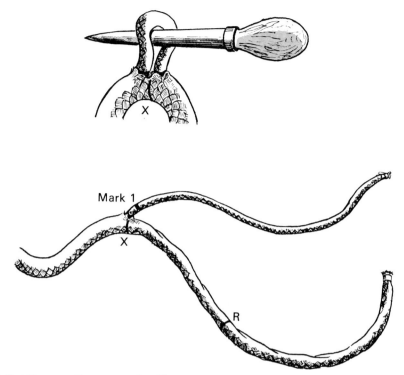

Mark 1

X

R

Fig. 6.41 Braidline eye splice – preparation (2)

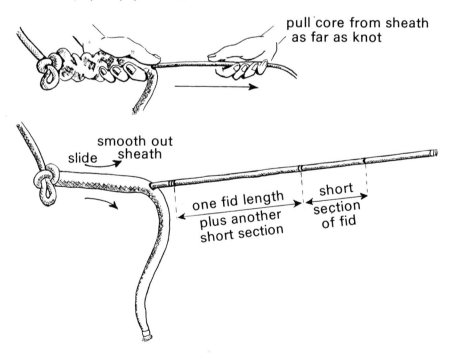

pull core from sheath
as far as knot

smooth out
slide   sheath

one fid length
plus another
short section

short
section
of fid

Fig. 6.42 Braidline eye splice – preparation (3)

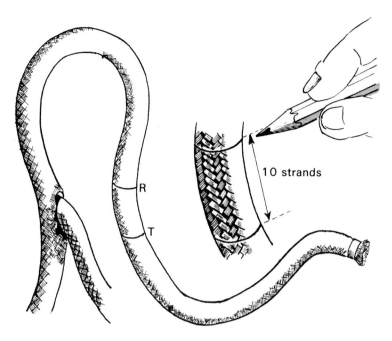

Fig. 6.43 Braidline eye splice – preparation (4)

the sheath with the pusher, and prise out the core (fig. 6.41). When the core is all out (from X to the end of the rope), bind the end of the core with adhesive tape.

Hold the core securely and slide the sheath back towards the knot (fig. 6.42) as far as possible, then work it forward again to eliminate all sheath slackness. Mark the core where it emerges from the sheath with an ink band called Mark 1. Slide the sheath back again from Mark 1, exposing more of the core and, from Mark 1, measure a 'short fid length' back along the core and make two pen marks – this is Mark 2. The term 'short fid length' refers to a length engraved on the Braidline splicing fid. From Mark 2 measure back a further fid length plus a short fid length and put three bands on to make Mark 3. All of these are shown in fig. 6.42.

Having so far made five marks, we have one more to make on the sheath before getting down to the real work of splicing. From point R, count 10 strands (to either left or

right) towards the end of the sheath and mark with ink a single band which will be referred to as point T. This process is detailed in fig. 6.43.

The first job in actually forming the eye splice is to insert the sheath into the core. To do this, the fid is inserted into the core at Mark 2 and brought out at Mark 3 (fig. 6.44). The taped end of the sheath is jammed into the hollow end of the fid and the pusher is then used to push both fid and sheath through the core and out at Mark 3. When the fid is removed, the rest of the sheath is pulled through the core until point T on the sheath meets Mark 2 on the core.

A similar process is used to feed the core into the sheath. The fid is inserted into the sheath at point T (fig. 6.45) and the core end is jammed into it. Use the pusher to work the fid and core down the sheath until they may be brought out at point X (fig. 6.46).

The vital cross-over joint has now been made and from this stage on it is more or

46

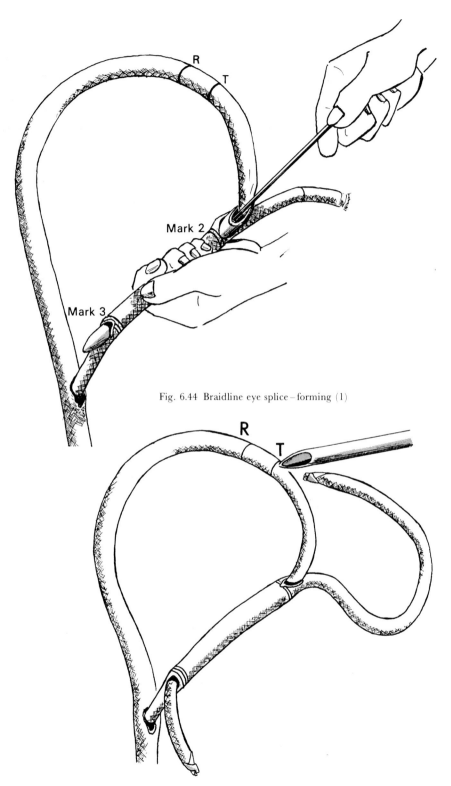

Fig. 6.44 Braidline eye splice – forming (1)

Fig. 6.45 Braidline eye splice – forming (2)

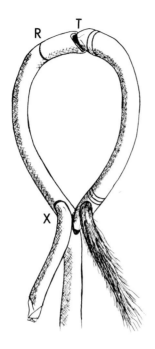

Fig. 6.46 Braidline eye splice – forming (3)

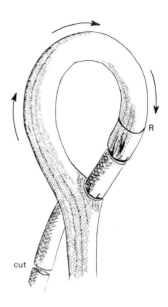

cut

Fig. 6.48 Braidline eye splice – forming (5)

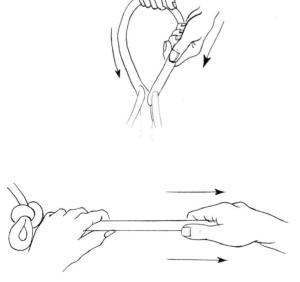

Fig. 6.47 Braidline eye splice – forming (4)

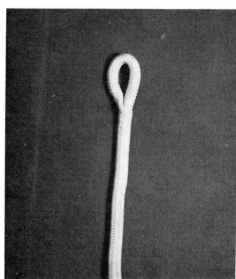

Fig. 6.49 Braidline eye splice – completion

less a tidying up job. Hold the core at Mark 3 and pull the sheath tail so that the core rucks up against the cross-over point. Remove the tape from the end of the sheath and unlay a length. Cut away some of the strands to taper the sheath (fig. 6.46). This tapered end can now be buried. Tighten up on the cross-over by pulling on the core tail at point X, then on the tapered sheath tail at Mark 3. Grip the cross-over tightly with one hand and use the other to smooth away all slack (fig. 6.47), working first towards point X, then towards Mark 3. The tapered sheath ends will disappear inside the core.

When the ends of the sheath have disappeared, start 'milking' the sheath towards the splice (fig. 6.47), pulling against the knot (which should be round a fixed object). You may be well advised to wear gloves while doing this, to avoid blisters. As the sheath is worked up, first Mark 3 will disappear, then Mark 2, followed by point T. Work as far as point R (fig. 6.48), and if bunching occurs at the cross-over point in the last stages, pull hard on the core tail to clear it.

All that remains to do now is to smooth out round the whole eye, cut off all but

$\frac{3}{4}$ to 1 in of the core tail (fig. 6.48), tuck it into the throat of the eye, smooth all round once more, and put on a tight whipping if you want to make it all tiddly. Finally, release the knot from about the cleat or fixed object. The finished eye is shown in fig. 6.49, without the whipping.

These instructions are complicated, but the work is not difficult provided each step is followed carefully. According to Bridon, the manufacturers of Braidline, this splice retains some 85 per cent of the strength of a new rope if done well.

Three-strand rope to wire splice

Many yachts have wire halyards with rope falls – either of Braidline type or three-strand pre-stretched polyester. The method of splicing Braidline to wire is explained on page 54: here we are dealing with splicing three-strand to wire.

First unlay the wire rope for a distance equal to about 30 diameters, and remove the heart if there is one. Put on a whipping round the rope where you stopped unlaying

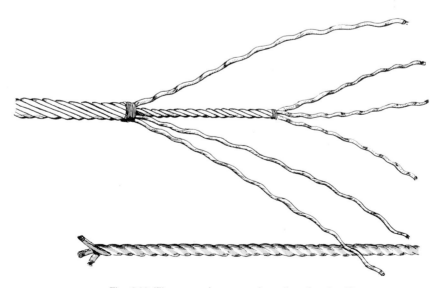

Fig. 6.50 Three-strand rope to wire splice – forming (1)

Fig. 6.51 Three-strand rope to wire splice – forming (2)

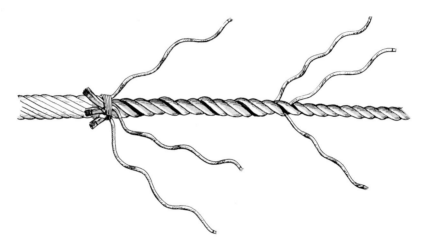

Fig. 6.52 Three-strand rope to wire splice – forming (3)

Fig. 6.53 Three-strand rope to wire splice – completion

it, and also on the end of each strand. Select three alternate strands and lay them up together for half their length. Apply a whipping where you stop. The wire should now be in the situation shown in fig. 6.50.

Next open up the end of the fibre rope, marry the strands with the three long wires (fig. 6.51) and seize them to the wire rope. Now worm the laid-up wire strands tightly into the rope as far as the whipping in the manner shown in fig. 6.51. When that is done and the wire has been worked well into the rope to form a core, only the ends should be sticking out as shown in fig. 6.52. To finish off, the wire is tucked over and under against the lay of the rope in the manner of a short splice (page 34) until the situation shown in fig. 6.53 is reached. At that point the ends are cut off and hidden in the lay of the rope, while the ends of the rope are also pared down. Finally the whole splice may be served by binding tightly with twine using either a serving board (see rackings and seizings, page 67) or a marlinspike and marlinspike hitch (page 69) to heave the turns taut.

Marlow sixteen-plait rope to wire tail splice

Nothing is so relentlessly efficient as the wire halyard, but then again, nothing is so hard on the hands. A plaited synthetic fibre rope by comparison is as limp and easy to handle as a string of sausages, and is very strong. Combine the benefits of the two with a rope to wire splice and you have the best of both worlds – a wire rope that does not stretch and offers minimum windage, and a soft rope which is easy to grip and make fast.

The wire should be either a 6 × 19 or a 6 × 37 construction and long enough to allow several turns around the winch. This is important because the rubbing of bare wire against the end of the splice as the halyard

is winched will chafe the splice and shorten its useful, safe life considerably. Incidentally, when measuring for the amount of wire rope, don't forget to add the amount needed to make the splice. Tools required are a hollow (Swedish) fid (although you might be able to get away with using an ordinary marlinspike), some sail twine, rigging tape, a sharp knife, and pliers.

The splice described here is designed for sixteen-plait Marlow polyester rope, and it is important to stick with this recommendation, because although other plaited or braided ropes may *look* similar, their construction will be different and each manufacturer will have their own, specifically designed splice. The wire used should be about half the diameter of the sixteen-plait rope and again, this recommendation is important, for otherwise great difficulty will be experienced in the second stage of the operation where the cover has to be slid over the primary splice.

Make a knot 6 ft (1.8 m) from the end to prevent the inner core of this two-part rope from being disturbed beyond the region of the splice. Slide back the outer cover to expose 48 in (1.2 m) of inner core. Cut off 6 in (150 mm) from the end of the inner core (fig. 6.54).

Tape the ends of each of the three strands of the inner core. Tape also the end of the wire which will need to be tapered. Take care with this operation because as the strands are cut progressively they will have a tendency to 'fly' apart and unstrand themselves. The taper should be about 9 in (225 mm) in length (fig. 6.55).

At a point 30 in (750 mm) from the end of the inner core, open up the lay and insert the end of the wire. Pass a few turns of tape around this point to hold the wire in position (fig. 6.56a).

Now carefully twist the wire into the lay of the rope with a spiralling action which will automatically bring the wire into the centre of the rope. Continue laying the wire

51

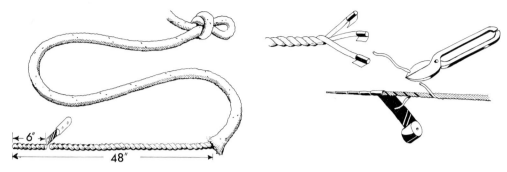

Fig. 6.54 Sixteen-plait rope to wire splice (1)　　　Fig. 6.55 Sixteen-plait rope to wire splice (2)

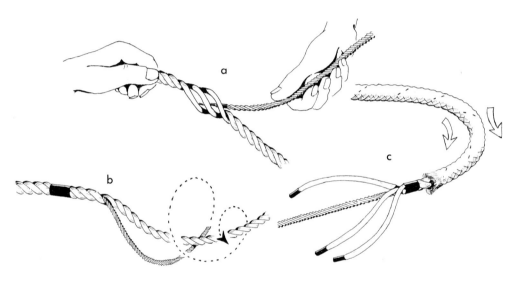

Fig. 6.56 Sixteen-plait rope to wire splice (3)

to a point 8 in (200 mm) from the end of the rope and tape at this point (fig. 6.56b).

Slide the outer cover over the inner core until this taped position is reached (fig. 6.56c).

The three strands of the inner core are now spliced into the wire *against* the lay. This means to say that the rope is tucked 'under and over' fashion rather like the ordinary rope eye splice with the fundamental difference that here *two* strands of wire are lifted instead of one as in the rope splice. Complete the first round of tucks passing each strand of rope under two strands of wire then repeat same until three rounds of tucks have been put in (fig. 6.57).

The fourth and fifth tucks are tapered so for this take out a number of yarns from each strand and tuck the remainder. Finally cut off the ends (fig. 6.58).

This completes the first part of the splice and the operation now is to splice the outer cover into the wire so that each of the two parts of the rope are individually spliced into the wire. Slide the outer cover over the splice and pass a tight whipping around the

52

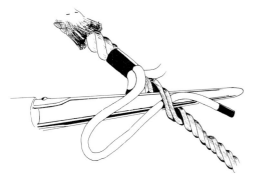

Fig. 6.57 Sixteen-plait rope to wire splice (4)

Fig. 6.60 Sixteen-plait rope to wire splice (7)

Fig. 6.58 Sixteen-plait rope to wire splice (5)

Fig. 6.61 Sixteen-plait rope to wire splice (8)

Fig. 6.59 Sixteen-plait rope to wire splice (6)

point where the inner splice finishes. Unlay the remaining part of the outer cover into separate yarns and divide into three. Tape the ends (fig. 6.59).

The outer cover is spliced into the wire *with* the lay. This is distinct from splicing against the lay and in practice what happens is that the rope strand is made to spiral around the wire strands which it is initially tucked under. Splicing with the lay completely buries the wire and produces a

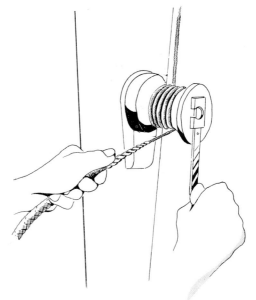

Fig. 6.62 Sixteen-plait rope to wire splice (9)

far neater appearance. Push the fid under two wire strands as previously, but this time pass the rope strand through from the opposite direction. Complete one round of tucks like this, but when attempting the second round, be very sure to tuck the same rope strands under the same two wire strands you started with (fig. 6.60).

The splice should develop a neat 'spiral' appearance; if it looks considerably different from the drawing or if the wires are seen to cross the rope strands, then you have not followed the correct sequence of tucking the same rope under the same two wire strands. Five tucks are required to complete this splice and with each round remove a yarn from the rope to produce a tapered appearance (fig. 6.61).

Cut off the ends and the splice is now complete (fig. 6.62).

Braidline to wire splice

Though several steps are involved in this procedure, it is a surprisingly simple technique. What happens is that first the core of the Braidline is spliced into the wire, and afterwards the sheath is spliced into it, giving a 'double' splice.

Materials needed are: wire (in this case 6 mm diameter 6×19 galvanized was used); Braidline (here it's a 10 mm diameter Super Polyester Braidline); sharp knife; hollow or 'Swedish' fid; Marina Braidline splicing fid (a pointed tube for threading rope or wire through, which is not absolutely essential but does make life easier); roll of adhesive tape. (See fig. 6.33.)

First step is to tie a knot in the rope about 2 metres from the end, fixing it to a solid object such as a cleat. Whip the end of the wire with tape and put a tape marking band roughly 40 cm along from the end. This marker is the point to which the wire will be buried inside the rope and is shown in fig. 6.33.

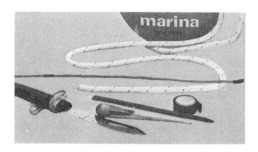

Fig. 6.63 Braidline to wire splice – forming (1)

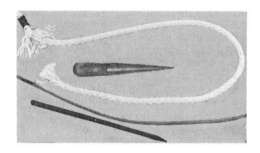

Fig. 6.64 Braidline to wire splice – forming (2)

Fig. 6.65 Braidline to wire splice – forming (3)

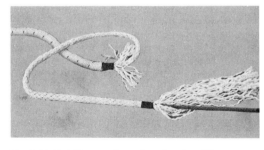

Fig. 6.66 Braidline to wire splice – forming (4)

Fig. 6.67 Braidline to wire splice – forming (5)

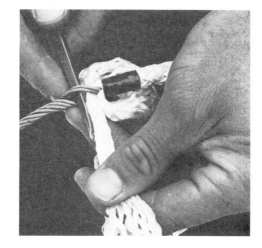

Fig. 6.69 Braidline to wire splice – forming (7)

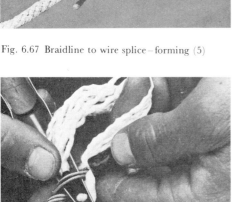

Fig. 6.68 Braidline to wire splice – forming (6)

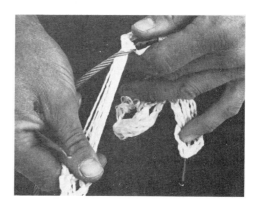

Fig. 6.70 Braidline to wire splice – forming (8)

Lightly whip the rope with tape 2 or 3 cm from the end and fray the strands, separating core and sheath by sliding the core back towards the knot. Figure 6.64 shows core and sheath separated with about a metre of core exposed.

The Marina Braidline splicing fid is inserted into the core (it should slide in easily, so don't force it), and the wire is inserted through the fid, up to the tape marker. Figure 6.65 shows this being done. Overlap the marker tape slightly with the frayed rope ends and grip them there with one hand. Pull the splicing fid out of the core

leaving the wire buried inside it.

Next tape the core firmly to the wire inside it about 15 cm back from the wire marker, and unlay the ends of the core to this new tape. Figure 6.66 shows the position now.

The long rope strands are now divided into three bunches and their ends whipped with tape as shown in fig. 6.67. Now you are ready to make the first splice.

Pass the Swedish fid under two strands of the wire close to the tape binding the core and wire, and pass one of the bunches of core strands down the hollow of the fid

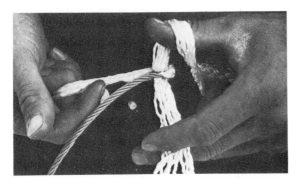

Fig. 6.71 Braidline to wire splice – forming (9)

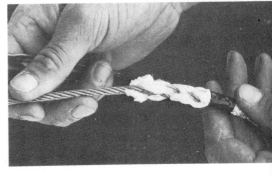

Fig. 6.73 Braidline to wire splice – forming (11)

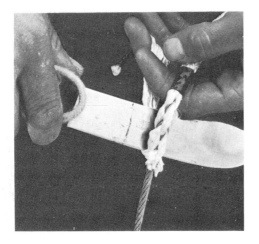

Fig. 6.72 Braidline to wire splice – forming (10)

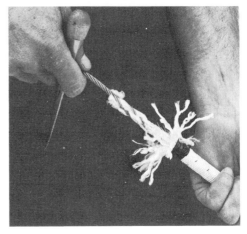

Fig. 6.74 Braidline to wire splice – forming (12)

under the wires (fig. 6.68). This is the first tuck. Make sure the wires are re-laid as smoothly as possible, and follow round the wire picking up the next two strands with the Swedish fid. Tuck the next bunch of core strands (fig. 6.69) and again re-lay the wire smoothly. The third tuck (fig. 6.70) is made the same way, and the first complete round is pulled tight (fig. 6.71). Three full tucks should be made in this way with each bunch of core strands, always trying to disturb the wire as little as possible.

Once all three tucks are completed the excess of rope strands is cut off (fig. 6.72). The result should be a neat splice between core and wire, as seen in fig. 6.73. That is the core of the Braidline dealt with – now we move on to the sheath.

First step for the sheath is to work it up over the spliced core, making sure not to leave any 'slack'. This is done as in fig. 6.74, by 'milking' the sheath over the core, pulling against the knot that was formed about a fixed object at the start.

With all of the sheath worked up, it is bound tightly to the wire with tape where the core splice finishes. This can be seen in fig. 6.75. The core is then unlayed and divided into three bunches in exactly the same way as the core was. It is then spliced

Fig. 6.75 Braidline to wire splice – completion

Fig. 6.76 Flemish wire eye splice (1)

into the wire (fig. 6.75), again in exactly the same way as was the core. A fourth tuck may be added using only half of each bunch, the rest of the strands having been cut out, to taper the splice and neaten it.

That completes the Braidline to wire splice and it only remains to parcel it with tape.

Fig. 6.77 Flemish wire eye splice (2)

Flemish wire eye splice

The Flemish wire eye splice is simplicity itself, as it does not involve any tucking, and the only tools required are wire cutters. The finished splice looks very neat and retains a high proportion of the wire rope's strength. It is suitable for any wire rope (such as 7×7 or 7×19) but not for 1×19.

To begin the eye splice, divide the wire, in this case a 7×19 wire rope, into two parts, one of three strands and the other of four including the straight heart strand. Tape the ends and unlay these two parts for at least four times the length of the required eye. Now cross one part over the other to form the size of eye you want (fig. 6.76), keeping the part with the core in it on the same side of the other part as it is at the

Fig. 6.78 Flemish wire eye splice (3)

throat of the eye where the wire is still laid up. This ensures that everything will knit together properly.

The part lying on top is taken back and passed up through the eye (fig. 6.77) and

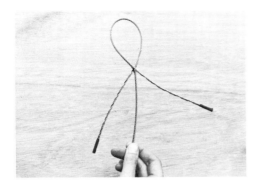

Fig. 6.79 Flemish wire eye splice (4)

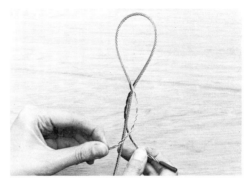

Fig. 6.81 Flemish wire eye splice (6)

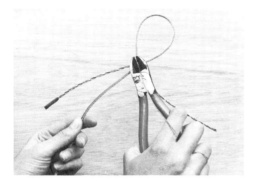

Fig. 6.80 Flemish wire eye splice (5)

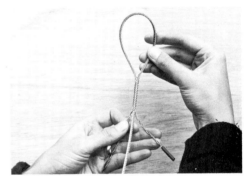

Fig. 6.82 Flemish wire eye splice (7)

settled into the empty groove in the other part. Continue this process of laying up on that side all the way down to the throat. Next take the other part, bring it forwards and pass it down through the eye (fig. 6.78) settling it into the empty groove as you did on the other side. Lay this side up all the way down to the throat as in fig. 6.79.

At this point the heart strand must be cut out using wire cutters (fig. 6.80) which, if they are not good cutters, can be an awkward job. Bury the cut ends inside the other strands so that no 'meat hooks' stick out to snag things. If a thimble is to be put in, it should be done at this point and the size of the eye itself should be adjusted if necessary by unlaying and re-laying it up.

Pull each part (now both consisting of three strands) back to its own side of the eye (fig. 6.81) and begin to lay them up

Fig. 6.83 Flemish wire eye splice (8)

together round the standing part of the wire (fig. 6.82). This must be done carefully, following the natural set of the strands and spiralling them round *together*.

When both parts have been laid up in this fashion they must be held securely with tape

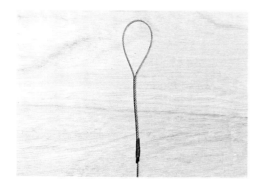

Fig. 6.84 Flemish wire eye splice (9)

(fig. 6.83), and putting that on is possibly the trickiest part of the splice as the wires want to spring undone. Tame them though and the splice should look like that in fig. 6.84. The splice is now usable, but for additional strength it would be as well to serve it over with wire or strong line up to the throat.

Wire eye splice (Liverpool splice)

The eye splice described here is only one of many varieties which can be used in wire. It is made in either 6×19 or 7×7 wire rope (which may also be referred to occasionally as 6×7 rope); splicing 1×19 strand also used for yacht rigging) is beyond the scope of all but a few amateur riggers, and is normally fitted with special terminals to avoid the need for a splice. The splice we are talking about here then is a straightforward splice tucked *with the lay* and has no locking turns. It is known as the Liverpool splice. Because there are no locking turns it is not suitable for such heavy work as crane wires or derrick runners, where continual twisting may cause it to unlay, but for yacht standing rigging it is perfectly suitable, and is found by many people to be easier than the over-and-under splice similar to the rope eye splice which is tucked against the lay.

Begin by putting on a whipping about

two feet from the end of the wire where the throat of the eye will be made. The next stage is to unlay the wire carefully up to the whipping and to separate the six working strands. Each of these strands will in turn have to be whipped although it is possible to short-cut this by either giving their ends a sharp twist with a pair of pliers, or by using adhesive tape.

Running through the centre of a 7×7 wire rope will be seen the core or heart. It may either be wire or tarred rope. It is best to cut this out to save complications, although experienced riggers invariably leave it in and bury it in the splice; removal does not significantly affect the strength of the rope.

This particular splice has a thimble and if this is to be put in then you will need to clamp the wire tightly around it (it is best squeezed up in a vice) and put on seizings at the shoulders and at the crown.

Figure 6.85 shows the spike driven in through the standing part of the wire and dividing it so that there are three strands to the right of it and three strands, plus the rope heart, to the left. The photo also shows the first tuck where the nearest or extreme right-hand strand has been passed beneath the three lifted strands.

The next stage is to withdraw the spike slightly so that the end strand drops off and only two strands remain to the right (on top) of it. Now take the next working strand in rotation and pass this beneath the spike. Draw the spike back again so the second strand drops off (fig. 6.86) and again pass the next working strand beneath the spike.

Figure 6.87 shows this stage of the splice complete where each of the first three working strands emerges between their respective strands on the standing part. At this juncture it is a good idea to pull the splice tight, and the best way is to remove it from the vice, hold the ends of the working strands in one hand and hammer the standing part of the wire with the head of the

59

Fig. 6.85 Wire eye splice – forming (1)

Fig. 6.86 Wire eye splice – forming (2)

Fig. 6.87 Wire eye splice – forming (3)

Fig. 6.88 Wire eye splice – forming (4)

spike. Some riggers prefer to continue tucking these three strands at this stage as they then hold the splice tight. However for the sake of clarity we will move on to the fourth tuck.

Figure 6.88 shows the fourth working strand tucked under its corresponding strand on the standing part. The remaining two strands follow this sequence, i.e. number 5 strand will pass under the fifth strand and number 6 will be tucked under the sixth. In fig. 6.89 the first row of tucks has now been completed and the splice has been drawn up tight.

When tucking *with the lay* (as opposed to tucking under and over fashion) each working strand is wrapped spirally around the strand which it is presently tucked beneath.

The quickest way to do this and a method which avoids confusion is to complete the five or six tucks necessary with each strand before moving on to the next. Whereas for the first round of tucks we drove the spike in from the left-hand side we must now drive it in *from the right*.

It is almost impossible to make the second tuck immediately above the first without distorting the wire, so the answer is to drive the spike in from the right and then twist it back up the standing part of the wire. The action of this is to lift the relevant strand in a position where it will be easier to tuck. Indeed the higher up the wire that the spike is taken the easier it will be to tuck the strand, but it is important however *to follow the turns of the spike with the working strand so*

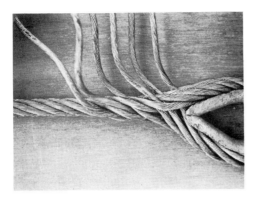

Fig. 6.89 Wire eye splice – forming (5)

Fig. 6.91 Wire eye splice – completion

Fig. 6.90 Wire eye splice – forming (6)

that each will pass around the wire the same number of turns. It is also important to ensure that the working strand is tucked *towards the point of the spike.* The next stage is to pull the strand tight while at the same time twisting the spike back down the wire so that the tuck finishes up immediately above the first one. Do not force either the spike or the strand in this operation, or it will distort the whole splice. Figure 6.90 shows the spike having been rotated up the wire and the working strand also; notice it is tucked *towards* the point of the spike.

Generally $5\frac{1}{2}$ tucks are sufficient for small work which means that three strands will have 5 tucks and the remaining three will have 6 tucks. This makes an average of $5\frac{1}{2}$

and the purpose of it is that they will then all emerge at the same place in the wire.

When all the tucks have been completed the splice must be hammered-up. Start close to the thimble and with the head of the spike carefully hammer the strands up the splice twisting the wire as you go. The purpose of this is to tighten the splice by driving all the slack to the top. Finally cut off the ends with a cold chisel and remove the seizings. Figure 6.91 shows the completed Liverpool splice.

Neatening the splice is made a little easier if, as each strand is tucked, it is given a half twist against its lay to flatten it out.

Talurit or Nicopress splicing and swageless terminals

Much of today's smaller yacht standing rigging is not spliced into thimble eyes at each end, but is held by a metal collar clamped tightly around the standing part and the end just above the thimble. This system is generally referred to in Great Britain as Talurit and in America as Nicopress splicing.

To avoid problems of electrolytic action, or at least to reduce them to a minimum, collars of alloy are used on galvanised wire and ones of copper on stainless-steel rigging.

Both act in exactly the same way, in that they are fitted over the wire and squeezed tightly in a hydraulic press until the metal is forced into the gaps between the strands and the two parts of the wire are held securely. Great care has to be taken not to part any of the outer strands in the standing part of the stay at either the top or bottom of the sleeve or collar as this would seriously affect the long-term strength of the wire.

Whilst the system is well suited to 7×7 wire rope of moderate size, as shown in fig. 6.92, it should only be used on the *smaller* sizes of 1×19 strand which has much less flexibility. A much better terminal for 1×19 wire is the swageless Norseman Terminal shown in fig. 6.93. There are of course other branded terminals but they all follow the same principle. The wire is passed through the body of the fitting and a cone is driven down over the inner strands. The outer ones

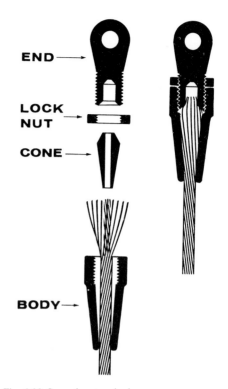

END

LOCK NUT

CONE

BODY

Fig. 6.93 Swageless terminal

are wrapped over the cone and the ends securely nipped in above it by screwing down the end into the body of the terminal. Finally a locking nut holds the whole fitting tight.

Bulldog splice

This is unquestionably the simplest way of putting an eye splice in wire rope. As with the Talurit or Nicopress splice it is possible to use it with 1×19 wire strand (telegraph-type wire), but not so satisfactorily.

The rope is bent round the thimble and the end is held against the working part as shown in fig. 6.94 with three bulldog clips. That's all there is to it, but there are three things to watch: the thimble (as with any splicing method) must have a big radius;

Fig. 6.92 Talurit splicing

the load; the bulldogs must be tightened in a 'tight, tighter, tightest' pattern, that is to say with the one nearest the thimble being put on tightly, the next one up being tightened down hard, and the top one being screwed up all the way.

Three-strand rope to chain splice

This splice is used to join a line to a length of chain – for instance a kedge warp to the chain on the anchor – when the rope is of too large a diameter to pass through the links of the chain. It is also used if the chain/warp joint has to render through a navel pipe.

The line is unlaid for half a dozen turns or so, the ends of the strands are whipped, and two of them are passed through the last link of chain. The third strand is unlaid a further half-dozen turns (fig. 6.95) and one of the other two strands is laid in its place.

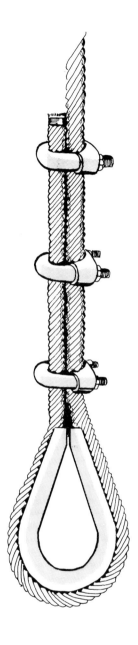

Fig. 6.94 Bulldog splice

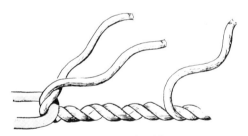

Fig. 6.95 Chain splice – forming (1)

Fig. 6.96 Chain splice – forming (2)

the bulldogs must be put on with their threaded ends on the standing part because the crown of the U part tends to bite in and cripple the wire, which obviously must not happen on the standing part which bears

Fig. 6.97 Chain splice - completion

This is done in the same way as for the long splice (page 35), taking one strand out and replacing it with a strand from the working part, turn for turn – again the diagram shows several turns unlaid just for clarity. The two ends are then knotted together (fig. 6.96) with an overhand knot (page 3), halved, and tucked against the lay. The remaining strand is also tucked against the lay, and the result is shown in fig. 6.97.

Marlow Multiplait to chain splice

Tools for the job: see fig. 6.98.

Unlay the four pairs of Multiplait strands for a distance equivalent in length to twelve links of chain and apply a strong whipping (fig. 6.99). Hold the rope so that you are looking directly into the heart of it and you will notice that of the four pairs there is one at the top, one at the bottom and two pairs in the middle which are crossed. It is these

crossed pairs in the centre with which you commence the first tuck. To help identify correctly they will either *both* have the black thread running through them or they will *both* be plain. It matters not just so long as they are both the same, i.e. both black or both plain.

Unlay each of these centre pairs into their two composing strands and tuck them through the first link of the chain in the manner described in the drawing (fig. 6.100). Two strands enter the link from below and two from above, and the important thing is that they are crossed (fig. 6.101).

Commence second tuck laying strands along either side of first link and tuck into second link in same manner (fig. 6.102). Pull the strands tight and you will notice that they will lay automatically on either side of the links as shown in the drawing, as shown in fig. 6.103. It may be helpful at this stage to lay the strands out of the way onto the body of the rope while you concentrate on the next link for tucking.

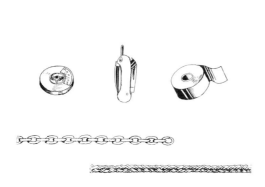

Fig. 6.98 Multiplait nylon to chain splice (1)

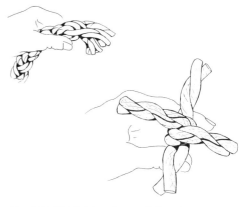

Fig. 6.99 Multiplait nylon to chain splice (2)

64

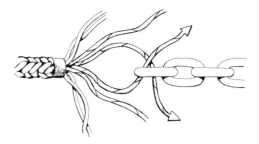

Fig. 6.100 Multiplait nylon to chain splice (3)

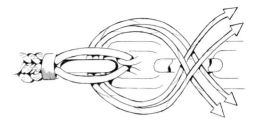

Fig. 6.104 Multiplait nylon to chain splice (7)

Fig. 6.101 Multiplait nylon to chain splice (4)

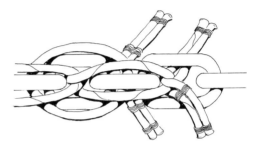

Fig. 6.105 Multiplait nylon to chain splice (8)

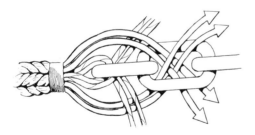

Fig. 6.102 Multiplait nylon to chain splice (5)

Fig. 6.106 Multiplait nylon to chain splice (9)

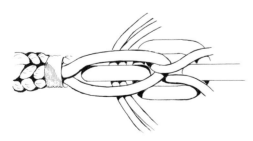

Fig. 6.103 Multiplait nylon to chain splice (6)

The third tuck is made by the first set of strands into the third link (fig. 6.104). The fourth tuck with the second set into the fourth chain link, and so on. Continue this alternating tucking until ten links have been completed (five with each pair).

Finish off by whipping the pairs as close to the links of chain as possible and heat seal the ends together as an extra precaution (fig. 6.105).

The completed splice (fig. 6.106).

65

Stitching ends together

If a halyard needs replacing, particularly one that is led inside the mast, the easiest way of replacing it is to stitch the end of the old halyard to the end of the new one and simply haul the old out and the new in.

A length of sail twine is half hitched around one strand, above the whipping, in either rope (fig. 6.107) and is stitched through behind one strand in the other rope, also above the whipping. Then a process similar to that for a needle-and-palm whipping (page 30) is carried out. The finished join is shown in fig. 6.108, where the lines form one continuous length with nothing to snag in the mast sheaves. The same method can be used just as well with plaited halyards of course. If both old and new halyards are synthetic, then an alternative to stitching is simply to fuse the two ends together with a match.

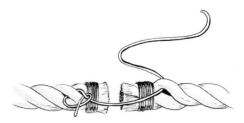

Fig. 6.107 Stitching ends together (1)

Fig. 6.108 Stitching ends together (2)

7 Seizings

It's something we hardly give credit for, but the ordinary wire or rope seizing, which can be applied in a matter of minutes at minimal cost, beats all the patent fastenings you can get. It was designed, probably, about the time when the early Egyptians were rigging their papyrus rafts and has been perfected by generations of seamen ever since. It is certainly now unlikely to be improved upon.

A seizing – i.e. the binding together of two ropes or spars to hold them secure – can be made from any kind of line – rope, wire, or small stuff; the size and type of material depends upon the requirements of the individual job. For example two spars can be lashed together quite effectively with rope but, if they are small and you have suitable wire which will really grip the wood hard, then obviously wire is better. Like all seamanship it is a matter of commonsense and using whatever materials are available.

But whichever material you choose it will first be necessary to work an eye in the end. If it is seizing wire then the eye is simply twisted; cod line (or rope) is spliced in an eye splice; small stuff such as marling, which is too fiddlesome to splice, is usually tucked back into its own lay. These three methods are shown in fig. 7.1.

Round seizing

A round seizing is begun by passing the seizing around both parts of the rope with the end coming up through the eye (fig. 7.2). Always be sure to work against the lay when seizing. This first turn is worked tight and it is followed by ten or a dozen turns around the parts of rope. They must be laid on really tightly, and to do this it is usual to use a serving board or mallet as shown in fig. 7.3. However, if you do not have a serving board, or there is not space to use one, the turns can be hauled tight with the aid of a marlinspike (fig. 7.4). A marlinspike hitch is formed in the seizing, and every third turn or so the spike is used to lever the turns tight. Figure 7.5 shows how the hitch is formed. Care should be taken to ensure

Fig. 7.1 Eyes in seizing stuffs

67

Fig. 7.2 Round seizing – forming (1)

Fig. 7.3 Round seizing – forming (2)

Fig. 7.4 Round seizing – forming (3)

that the load is on the correct side of the hitch – in this figure the load should be on the part going out of the picture to the right. It will also be noticed that the hitch conveniently falls apart immediately the spike is withdrawn, thus it cannot jam under load.

When the turns have duly been completed, a half hitch is formed around both rope parts to hold the turns tight, and a second layer of turns is now applied known as riding turns. These, shown in fig. 7.6, are applied only hand-tight, otherwise they would become buried in amongst the bottom set. Always use two less riding turns than the number of turns in the first layer. This prevents them falling off the ends.

The last riding turn is brought up through to the front by passing it between the two parts of rope and up through the original eye (fig. 7.7). Next, two or three 'frapping' turns are put on parallel to and between the ropes being seized together. Some effort should be made to pull these really tight using a marlinspike hitch. A

common way to apply frapping turns is to make them in the form of a clove hitch although this needs backing up, either by making an overhand knot in the end to prevent it pulling through, or by passing several turns around one rope part (fig. 7.8) and finishing off with half hitches or by tucking the end into the rope's lay.

An alternative method, shown in fig. 7.9, is simply to make half hitches around both parts of the frapping turns. Yet another method, and a certain way of pulling the frapping turns up tight, is to form a bight in the last frapping turn and pass the end back through it forming an overhand knot to stop the end pulling out again (fig. 7.10). The overhand knot could of course be re-

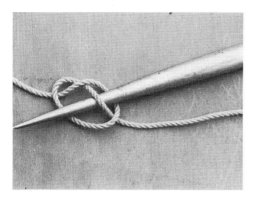
Fig. 7.5 Marlinspike hitch

Fig. 7.8 Round seizing – forming (6)

Fig. 7.6 Round seizing – forming (4)

Fig. 7.9 Round seizing – forming (7)

Fig. 7.7 Round seizing – forming (5)

Fig. 7.10 Round seizing – forming (8)

placed by a half hitch round the frapping turns (fig. 7.11), but it would have to be forced under, losing some of the tightness of the turns in the process.

The seizing is now complete and fig. 7.12 shows it finished off with the overhand knot worked tight. This then is known as a *round seizing* and is used wherever the strain on

Fig. 7.11 Round seizing – forming (9)

Fig. 7.14 Racking seizing – forming (2)

Fig. 7.12 Round seizing – completion

Fig. 7.15 Racking seizing – forming (3)

Fig. 7.13 Racking seizing – forming (1)

Fig. 7.16 Racking seizing – forming (4)

70

Fig. 7.17 Racking seizing – forming (5)

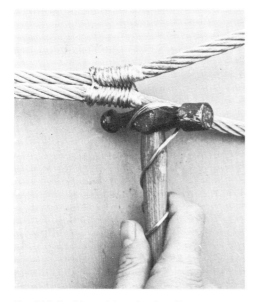

Fig. 7.18 Racking seizing – forming (6)

Fig. 7.19 Racking seizing – completion

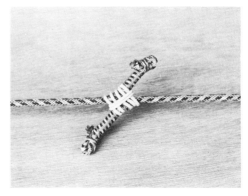

Fig. 7.20 Racking seizing – in use (1)

Fig. 7.21 Racking seizing – in use (2)

Fig. 7.22 Mole wrench used to hold wire

71

the ropes is from the same direction, i.e. it simply clamps the two parts of rope together. For a seizing of a less permanent nature the riding turns are omitted and this is known as a *flat seizing*.

Racking seizing

The racking seizing is used wherever the strain on the two ropes being seized together will come in opposite directions, or when excessive tension is expected on one part of the rope only.

The turns are laid on figure-of-eight fashion as in fig. 7.13, and are hove taut with a marlinspike. Ten or fifteen turns are usual, and in this case the riding turns are allowed to lie in between the initial turns. The seizing is finished off in the same way as a round seizing (page 67).

Racking seizings are commonly used with braided rope where splicing is difficult. Figure 7.14 shows such a seizing put on to hold the eye of a pair of headsail sheets. Note the seizing must be put on towards the eye to draw the throat in really tight.

In fig. 7.15 a racking seizing is being made with seizing wire around two small spars, and a hammer is being used to act

instead of a serving mallet to heave the turns taut. Then in fig. 7.16 it can be seen how the riding turns fit in between the figure-of-eight turns underneath, particularly when wire is used. This photo also shows how the seizing will be finished off in the same way as for rope.

Before a seizing can be put on wire rope, it is necessary to cover both parts with either canvas or rigging tape to prevent the turns of seizing wire slipping while they are applied. This can be seen in fig. 7.17, while fig. 7.18 shows the turns being tightened, again with a hammer. Finally fig. 7.19 shows the completed seizing.

Clearly a seizing can be used in a variety of ways, and in fig. 7.20 we see a racking seizing being used to secure lengths of elastic shock cord. Notice, by the difference in diameter between the parts under load and the lazy ends, how much weight has been applied and how little the seizing has distorted under the strain.

Instead of using a wire splice as described on page 59 a really tight racking seizing can be used to put a thimble in a wire rope – at least on a temporary basis – as can be seen in fig. 7.21. First, as for the splice, the thimble must be securely seized to the wire, and to do this it can be held there using a Mole wrench as shown in fig. 7.22.

8 Handling ropes

Coiling

There are three good reasons for coiling a rope down neatly: it is easier to use the rope again when needed quickly; it prevents it from becoming kinked; and it takes up less stowage space.

On most occasions we coil ropes in the hand, but however it is done always coil with the lay of the rope, which with a right-hand lay will mean clockwise. Take the end of the rope in one hand and begin to form loops, as shown in fig. 8.1, imparting a slight twist, *in the direction of the lay*, as each coil is formed.

A badly twisted rope, such as that shown in fig. 8.2, needs a lot of clearing and this one will have to be coiled a second time to get all the twist out. In an extreme case you may have to twirl the rope or even tow it astern to rid it of kinks.

When it comes to coiling Braidline core-and-sheath rope a different technique is followed. Here the rope has no inherent lay, and therefore no twist must be imparted to it. To avoid such twisting the coils are made in figures-of-eight, as shown in fig. 8.3. If the hand positions are compared with those in fig. 8.1, it will be seen that whereas with laid rope the hand is turned palm upwards to feed the rope into the other hand (thus twisting the rope), with Braidline it is kept palm downward, thus avoiding twist.

Coiling down on deck

There is naturally a physical limit to the amount and size of rope or line that can be held and coiled by hand. It will vary from person to person of course, but with ropes too large to coil by hand it is necessary to form the coils on the deck (or ground if ashore).

Begin by laying at least three turns flat on the deck as is being done in fig. 8.4, then build up from there in layers of three, working the coils out from the centre on one layer, and in from the edge on the next (fig. 8.5). In this way the coil will be kept solid and will neither fall over nor take up too much space (fig. 8.6).

Flaking down

It is often necessary to let a line out on the run, that is to say have it pay out quickly as might be the case with an anchor warp when letting go, and it could be dangerous to have it snarl up at the wrong moment. If you try to run a line out from a coil laid on deck it will foul up. The only way to ensure that a line runs freely is to flake it down beforehand.

To do this the line is laid out in a series of parallel loops like those shown in fig. 8.7. These loops are then crossed by a second

Fig. 8.1 Coiling (1)

Fig. 8.3 Coiling (3)

Fig. 8.2 Coiling (2)

layer of loops as in fig. 8.8, and if necessary further layers on top of these, each at right angles to the one below. The process is referred to as faking and snaking.

When flaking a line down remember to start from the inboard end: no line can be expected to run freely from the bottom of the pile!

Incidentally, the kedge warp shown in our figures has been connected directly to the anchor and not to an intermediate length of chain, simply for clarity and space saving. Normally there would be about three fathoms of chain in between warp and anchor.

Half-hitch coil

Untidy lines and ropes are sloppy and unseamanlike, but more than being untidy, an uncoiled rope can be dangerous. Wherever possible loose lines hanging from cleats should be 'made up'.

The quickest and simplest way to do this is to make a coil, starting close to the cleat

Fig. 8.4 Coiling on deck (1)

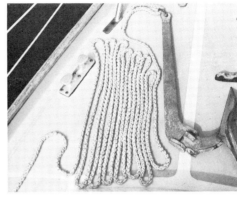

Fig. 8.7 Flaking down (1)

Fig. 8.5 Coiling on deck (2)

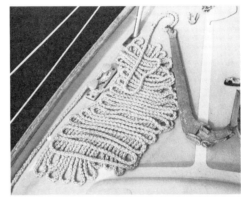

Fig. 8.8 Flaking down (2)

Fig. 8.6 Coiling on deck (3)

Fig. 8.9 Half-hitch coil (1)

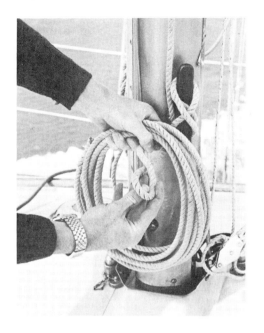

Fig. 8.10 Half-hitch coil (2)

Fig. 8.12 Half-hitch coil (4)

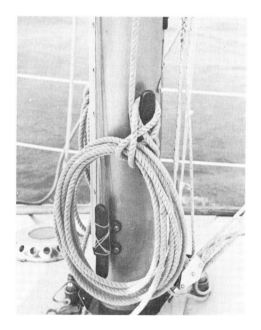

Fig. 8.11 Half-hitch coil (3)

Fig. 8.13 Half-hitch coil (5)

Fig. 8.14 Half-hitch coil for stowage (1)

Fig. 8.16 Half-hitch coil for stowage (3)

Fig. 8.15 Half-hitch coil for stowage (2)

and working towards the end (never in any circumstances coil a line towards the end made fast or a multitude of kinks will result).

When the line has been coiled hold it in the left hand and pass the right hand through the middle to grasp the rope close to where it leaves the cleat (fig. 8.9). Pull the rope through the middle of the coil and twist the loop which forms as in fig. 8.10. Then place this loop over the upper horn of the cleat and settle it down (fig. 8.11). If it is still too loose, simply put more turns in before hanging it on the cleat horn.

Very often the coil will hang more securely if the loop is wedged behind the standing part above the cleat (fig. 8.12), as the load on this pins the loop tight against the mast. A close view is shown in fig. 8.13.

Half-hitch coil for stowage

Perhaps the quickest and simplest method of making up a coil which is to be stowed

Fig. 8.17 Buntline coil (1)

Fig. 8.19 Buntline coil (3)

Fig. 8.18 Buntline coil (2)

Fig. 8.20 Buntline coil (4)

Fig. 8.21 Buntline coil (5)

is to make a half hitch round the top. This is popularly used when making up lines, heaving lines, etc., which will have to be carried and stowed in a deck locker or bosun's store. You should leave sufficient tail for a clove hitch to be made over a hook to hang the coil by. The half-hitch coil holds well, but is quick to let go and once released the line is immediately ready for use.

The first step is to make up the coil in the usual way and with the final few feet form a loop (fig. 8.14), then pass the end of the line back over the top of the coils and forward through the small loop (fig. 8.15). The half-hitch so formed is then settled (fig. 8.16) and the line is ready for stowage.

Buntline coil or gasket coil

Deriving its name from the buntlines on squaresails which, with one end permanently attached to the sails, had to be coiled and secured *in situ*, the buntline coil can either be used to hold a made-up rope

in position against a cleat or it can be used to make up a rope for stowage.

Begin by coiling the rope in the usual way, then wrap the remaining few feet around the coils (fig. 8.17). Take four or five turns, pass a loop through the upper part of the coil above these frapping turns (fig. 8.18), spread the loop and bring it forward over the top of the coil (fig. 8.19), then drop it down over them to lie on top of the frapping turns (fig. 8.20). When the slack is taken up it should look as in fig. 8.21.

The useful part about this way of securing a coil is that it is released simply by lifting the loop back off the top of the coil – no need to feed an end all the way through – and it can as we said be made with one end cleated or otherwise fixed.

Looking after rope

Rope, like all parts of a boat, needs care and attention; it is not indestructible. Though man-made fibre rope is impervious to attack by damp, and can safely be stowed away while still wet, natural fibre rope should be dried out fully in a normal atmosphere and stowed in well-ventilated lockers.

All rope must be kept clean and free from dirt, grit, or oil which is often picked up on mooring lines. Particularly after lying alongside a wharf, but in any case where rope is found to be dirty, wash thoroughly in clean fresh water, being careful not to use detergent on natural fibres; allow to dry in the open air. Remember too that splices and their servings are natural water traps.

Again rope does not like excessive heat and should be kept clear of boilers, flames, exhaust pipes and so on. Man-made fibres are particularly prone to damage by self-created heat when, for instance, they are surged too fast around a winch drum, so take it easy. Indeed some poor-quality synthetic rope, which does not contain inhibitors, may be degraded by prolonged

Fig. 8.22 Examples of chafe (1)

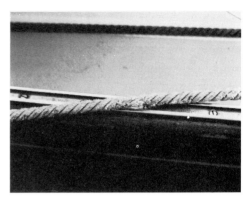

Fig. 8.24 Examples of chafe (3)

Fig. 8.23 Examples of chafe (2)

Fig. 8.25 Examples of chafe (4)

exposure to the ultra-violet radiation of sunlight. However, rope produced by reputable manufacturers should not suffer in this way.

While it is obvious that a sharp edge can tear at the fibres of a rope it should also be remembered that even moderately sharp turns, as for example with undersized cleats or sheaves, can also inflict damage by crippling the fibres. The radius of the groove in a sheave should always be a little bigger than that of the rope in it, and it should be deep enough to hide at least a third of the rope's circumference. It is recommended that the ratio of sheave to rope diameter should be at least 5 : 1, and for wire rope at least 12 : 1. Thus it will be noticed that a great many thimbles put in the ends of

rigging are ridiculously small, and some of the masthead sheaves for wire halyards are none too big either.

Do not allow kinks to remain in a rope, but remove them by coiling. Remember too they must have been induced by something. What? Find out and put it right. When using a new rope it will probably be difficult to coil initially since it will be stiff and tend

80

Fig. 8.26 Permanent mooring lines

Fig. 8.27 Anti-chafe method – using plastic tube

The line in fig. 8.24 has been sawing against a toerail fairlead track as the boat lies to her mooring. Figure 8.25 shows a boat about to lose her stern line for the simple reason that it has been given a totally unfair lead through the quarter fairlead.

When leaving a boat for long periods, as for example in a marina through the winter months, it is a good idea to shackle mooring lines to prevent them becoming chafed on the mooring cleats or bollards (fig. 8.26).

Probably the best anti-chafe method is to pass a length of plastic tube over the line (fig. 8.27) where it passes through the fairlead. This will greatly prolong the life of the warp, provided the tube stays put, and to ensure this it may actually have to be sewn in place. The fact that two warps are lying side by side does not matter because each is protected independently.

You, your family, or your boat may depend for its safety on the strength of a rope or line that is slowly chafing through. Be careful and never allow chafe to continue once it has been noticed.

to twist easily. It can be straightened out quite well by towing astern for a while.

Keep all lines away from chemicals – paint stripper, brush cleaner, toilet chemicals, etc. Nylon is resistant to attack by alkaline solutions, and polyester to the effects of acid, but neither is completely impervious and it is as well not to take chances.

By far the biggest problem where rope is concerned, is that of chafe (fig. 8.22) and the other figures show some of the places where it is most likely to occur. A great deal of care and attention is needed if chafe is to be avoided. Figure 8.23 shows a seemingly good siting of a large-diameter cheek block on the toerail, but there are three lines lying in it. Each one may move independently and so chafe against the next.

9 Rope seamanship

Cleating

The cleat is probably one of the fastest and most efficient methods of securing a line. It is designed so that turns can be put on or cast off quickly under load, but it can only make this possible if the rope is turned up in the correct manner.

An example of incorrect use is shown in fig. 9.1. Coming from the top of the photograph, the standing part, or the part under load, has been led first to the left of the forward edge of the cleat instead of the right of the back edge. Two things could now happen: either the standing part could ride across and jam the second turn making it impossible to throw it off in a hurry, or alternatively it will be difficult to snub the rope with one turn around the cleat, should this be necessary.

Cleats should be angled at 10–20 degrees to the direction of load on the line to be cleated. This is to ensure that the standing part is kept clear of the cleat and does not jam the subsequent turns. Figure 9.2 shows this. The standing part has been led correctly to the back edge of the cleat and no normal amount of movement in it can cause it to press tight against the other turns.

It is usual to make one complete turn around the cleat before putting on the figure-of-eight turns. The initial round turn assists when snubbing or paying out under

Fig. 9.1 Cleating – incorrect use

load. Exactly the same pattern is followed on twin bollards such as those shown in fig. 9.3 where the first round turn is being made. Figure-of-eight turns are laid on top of this as in fig. 9.4.

Many cleats fitted to boats today are not big enough to take sufficient turns to ensure that the line will not fall off, particularly some of the springier synthetic ones. To

Fig. 9.2 Cleating – angling to load on line

Fig. 9.3 Cleating – first round turn

Fig. 9.4 Cleating – figure-of-eight turns

overcome this, some people resort to the dubious practice of putting a final jamming turn on the cleat. *This practice is dangerous* as the last turn may jam under load, making it impossible to cast off quickly. If, however, you do decide to lay on a jamming turn (rather than fit a larger cleat), use a slipped half hitch as shown in fig. 9.5. Put this on in the same direction as the other turns and it will improve your chances of undoing it.

Securing to a staghorn

A staghorn is a bollard with a pair of horizontal arms to which mooring lines are made fast. The technique for securing to a staghorn is simple. The line is led round the bollard, up over one arm (fig. 9.6), back across the same side of the bollard and up over the other arm again figure-of-eight fashion (fig. 9.7). The sequence is continued as in fig. 9.8, until sufficient turns have been laid on and the rope is secured, as it is in fig. 9.9. This method allows the line to be cast off even while under load which, as with mooring lines, will often be the case.

Securing to a samson post

When securing a line to a samson post or mooring bollard we use a system often given the title 'no-name' knot. A series of turns is taken round the samson post and a bight of rope (or chain) is passed under the load part (fig. 9.10) and dropped over the turns on the post. The end can then be taken round the post again and another bight passed under the standing part to be dropped in turn over the post. This process can be repeated as often as desired.

There is nothing in this no-name knot to jam, and so it is ideal for making up an anchor chain or mooring warp which will have to be freed while still under load. *Never*

Fig. 9.5 Cleating – using slipped half hitch

on any account take a turn round the post with the load-bearing part, only use the lazy end. Figures 9.11 and 9.12 show the no-name knot being used on a windlass barrel where it will work just as well as on a samson post or bollard.

Bosun's chair and gantline hitch

When it is necessary to go up the mast, whether to repair something or just to inspect, the most usual method is to use a bosun's chair. This often takes the form of a wooden board suspended in a rope strop (fig. 9.13), and attached to the fall of a halyard. (If the halyard is considered too weak for any reason or too small, then a gantline will have to be rove in its place.)

The wood is drilled at each corner and the rope is passed up from the underside through one hole, down through the hole on the same long side, across and up through the one diagonally opposite, then finally down through the remaining hole before being spliced to the first end with a

Fig. 9.6 Securing to staghorn (1)

Fig. 9.7 Securing to staghorn (2)

Fig. 9.8 Securing to staghorn (3)

short splice. This results in two parallel loops above – like the handles of a shopping basket – and a crossover on the underside. The line is seized beneath the board where it crosses, and this and the splice are shown in fig. 9.14. Finally the two loops are seized together above the board as shown in fig. 9.13.

84

Fig. 9.9 Securing to staghorn (4)

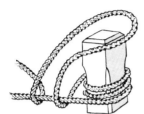

Fig. 9.10 Securing to samson post

Fig. 9.11 Securing to windlass (1)

The halyard fall is bent to the eye of the slings either by using a double becket bend or a shackle. The person going up the mast then sits in the chair and all is set for him to be hoisted, or to hoist himself, to wherever he needs to work.

When hauling someone up the mast do be extremely careful to keep plenty of turns on the winch drum, and always *make fast* as soon as you stop hauling. Also never stand under a man working aloft except while hauling. If he dropped anything it could hurt you quite badly. If circumstances permit, have another man watching him while you watch the turns on the winch.

If the man aloft is going to be occupied for some time, he can release the person on deck for other business by tying a gantline hitch or self-lowering hitch with the halyard fall. This hitch allows him to control his descent or to stay in one place as he chooses.

To form the gantline hitch he squeezes the halyard fall and working part together with one hand and with the other he reaches through the chair strops as in fig. 9.15 and takes hold of the fall. He pulls

Fig. 9.12 Securing to windlass (2)

Fig. 9.13 Bosun's chair (1)

Fig. 9.15 Bosun's chair – using gantline hitch (1)

Fig. 9.14 Bosun's chair (2)

Caution
It is a sensible safety precaution to tie yourself into a bosun's chair or to rig a backstrap so that you cannot fall out.

Fig. 9.16 Bosun's chair – using gantline hitch (2)

Fig. 9.17 Bosun's chair – using gantline hitch (3)

Fig. 9.19 Bosun's chair – using gantline hitch (5)

Fig. 9.18 Bosun's chair – using gantline hitch (4)

Fig. 9.20 Bosun's chair – using gantline hitch (6)

Fig. 9.21 Bosun's chair – using gantline hitch (7)

Fig. 9.22 Tailing on winches – mast winch (1)

through a large bight of it and passes this over his head and body (fig. 9.16). He takes it all the way over (fig. 9.17), until it is hanging down as in fig. 9.18, at which time he swops hands to get the other arm through the bight before working his feet through (fig. 9.19). The bight is then brought up to the top of the strops and is shortened down (fig. 9.20). The hitch is worked tight, and he may now let go with both hands (fig. 9.21). To lower himself down all he has to do is slacken off the hitch and work some of the fall through. If in doing so he should slip his grip he will be brought up very quickly.

Do not try to make this hitch in wire rope as it will cripple it.

Tailing on winches

It is not sufficient to slap three or four turns on a winch, crank the handle, and expect very much to happen. Obviously you need to haul on the lazy end to prevent the turns from slipping. This is called 'tailing on the winch'. It can either be done singularly

Fig. 9.23 Tailing on winches – mast winch (2)

88

with one person using his free hand, or, if the weight on the sheet or whatever is excessive, then another person may be employed to do the tailing.

Figure 9.22 shows a halyard fall being hauled on round a mast winch, while fig. 9.23 shows one person both winching in with his left hand and tailing on the halyard fall with his right.

In the case of sheet winches, the slack in the sheet is hauled in, then a turn is taken on the drum (fig. 9.24), followed by a second (fig. 9.25), and at least a third (fig. 9.26). Then the sheet is properly hardened in either, as in fig. 9.27, by one person tailing with one hand and winching in with the other, or if the manpower is available, by one person winching and another tailing as in fig. 9.28, taking care not to get in each other's way.

Once someone has begun to winch in, never pull on the sheet or halyard ahead of the winch as this will certainly cause trouble, probably a riding turn. Also, when tailing, keep your hands well away from the winch just in case something slips; and don't leave handles in winches as they are a nuisance when casting off turns and if a ratchet slips they could break your ribs.

Riding turns

A riding turn is the description given to a snarl-up on a winch barrel when a lower or inside turn 'rides up' and sits on top of its adjacent turns thus making further winching impossible. It happens as in fig. 9.29 where the lazy end on the left has become trapped under the turns of the load part on the right. This mess may well be caused by someone hauling on a sheet ahead of the winch, or by putting too many turns round the barrel of the winch before the slack in the sheet is taken up, or by winching in when the sheet is still flogging about.

How do we clear a riding turn? If there is no weight on the rope and no necessity to hold it, then the riding turn is best cleared if possible by hauling on the lazy end and so unwinding the turns. Alternatively the load on the rope can be held by some independent means while the mess on the winch is cleared. This system, however, must be able to exert a considerable force because the weight has to be taken off the standing part so that it is slack at the winch. If chance has set things up conveniently it may be possible to apply a stopper (as discussed on page 22) and take the load on a more powerful winch, but this is not to be counted on as a likely possibility. The method with the greatest chance of success is undoubtedly the one using a Spanish windlass.

Just before we talk about its application here, let's see its more common role as shown in fig. 9.30 where it is being used to draw the two parts of a steel hawser together. Its layout is quite easy to follow and its principle is similarly straightforward. By turning the two marlinspikes in the direction of the arrows the bar is also turned and the line wound up round it. As this line is wound up it naturally heaves the two parts of the hawser together. It is an extremely powerful set-up, and with a little adaptation is just what we want for clearing a riding turn.

A stopper is clapped on the standing part of the sheet ahead of the winch and led aft to a convenient point where a bar can be held across the side deck at right angles to the sheet and stopper. The stopper is looped around this bar and a marlinspike inserted in the loop in the way shown in fig. 9.31. The lazy end (bottom of the picture) is held taut to pin the marlinspike which is then revolved slowly until the load on the sheet is transferred to the stopper. Then the riding turn can be unmuddled. Figure 9.32 shows the set-up in use. Where possible it is better to use something larger than a marlinspike for greater purchase.

Fig. 9.24 Tailing on winches – sheet winch (1)

Fig. 9.26 Tailing on winches – sheet winch (3)

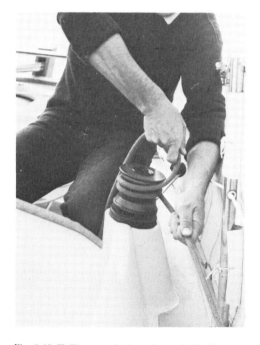

Fig. 9.25 Tailing on winches – sheet winch (2)

Fig. 9.27 Tailing on winches – sheet winch (4)

Fig. 9.28 Tailing on winches – sheet winch (5)   Fig. 9.29 Riding turn

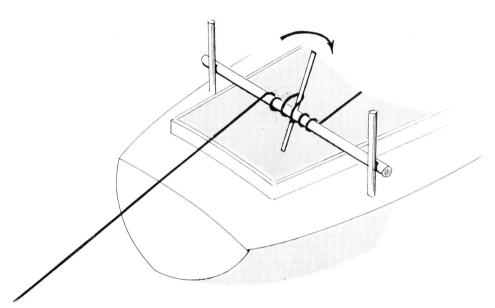

Fig. 9.30 Spanish windlass in use to haul boat astern, e.g. when kedging off

Surging a rope

If you are coming into an alongside berth the first line to get ashore is generally the stern line so that a turn can be snatched on a bollard and the way taken off the boat. It sounds easy and usually it is, but you have to watch out or else one day the boat will be travelling faster than you thought, and either you'll be pulled into the water or you'll lose a finger or two trapped between the rope and the bollard. To avoid this you will have to learn to surge the line.

Initially a full turn is taken, keeping hands well away, and then as the load comes on, the line must be eased away or

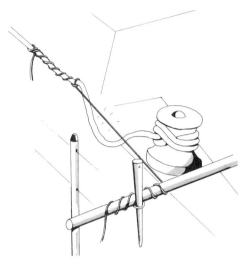

Fig. 9.33 Surging sheet round winch

Fig. 9.31 Clearing a riding turn by using a Spanish windlass

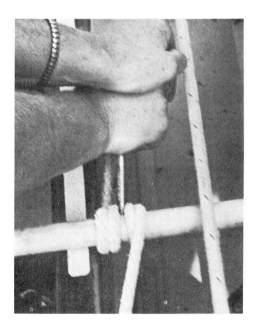

Fig. 9.32 Riding turn using Spanish windlass (2)

surged round the bollard, post, cleat or whatever. This way the boat is brought gently to a halt. If you turned the rope up immediately, the snatch load could part the line, but don't surge it too fast either as that

way you could lose control and see the end disappear, or the frictional heat could damage the rope. Once the strain is off and the boat has been brought to a halt, then the line can be hardened in and made up properly.

There are many occasions when you will have to surge a line, such as when anchoring with ropes or when starting a sheet, but the golden rule is to keep your hands and especially your fingers clear – they are far more precious than a replaceable boat or rope. Figure 9.33 shows the way to surge a sheet round a winch, using the heel of the hand to put pressure on the turns while keeping the fingers outstretched and well clear.

Heaving line

The primary purpose of the heaving line is to assist big ships in docking; they use it as a 'messenger' to send their heavier lines ashore. Many smaller craft do not carry heaving lines although they can be immensely useful at times. Few of us for example can throw a mooring line 50 feet into the eye of the wind, and yet this could become necessary when passing a line to a stranded vessel. Similarly, it is most difficult

Fig. 9.34 Heaving line (1) – coiling

Fig. 9.35 Heaving line (2) – swinging

to land an ordinary line within the grasp of a man in the water, or to somebody in a dinghy with a broken oar.

A more common situation is when you are required to throw an unweighted line 30 feet up the side of a quay, when all you can see is sky and the soles of the harbour master's boots. You may not need a heaving line very often, but it is something you can ill afford to be without.

Throwing a heaving line is a minor skill with the emphasis on direction rather than vast range. It is a common practice to throw the line overarm because this seems to promise greater power, but if the line is thrown this way the coils cannot unwind freely and they often overtake the weighted end and bring it down prematurely. Heaving lines are best thrown underhand when the coils will come away cleanly and with much more control and accuracy. The range can be increased with practice, but in most cases direction and a clear run are much more important.

The technique is first of all to coil half the

Fig. 9.36 Heaving line (3) – throwing

93

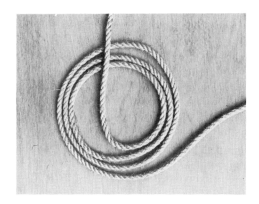

Fig. 9.37 Monkey's fist – forming (1)

Fig. 9.39 Monkey's fist – forming (3)

Monkey's fist

Heaving lines can be made with any rope although it is a definite advantage if you can use one which will float. If you are making a heaving line from new rope it is advisable to stretch it for a couple of days before use so that it will lose its stiffness and resultant tendency to kink. The line should be no bigger than about 10 millimetres ($\frac{13}{32}$-inch) in diameter and between 10 and 12 fathoms in length.

The traditional terminal knot for a heaving line is the monkey's fist. The advantage of this knot is that a small wooden or rubber ball can form the central core of the knot and this will give the end of the line added weight to make it carry further. A wooden ball also helps to make the line float – important when throwing to a man in the water.

To make the monkey's fist, form three loops as in fig. 9.37 about four feet from the

Fig. 9.38 Monkey's fist – forming (2)

line into large bights, at least two feet in diameter, then the second half is coiled in much smaller loops. These coils and the weighted end are held in your throwing hand, as in fig. 9.34. Holding the coil at your side a few swings to and fro can be made to gain momentum (fig. 9.35), before throwing (fig. 9.36).

94

end of the rope. Next, with the working end, pass three loops around the original three but at right angles to them (fig. 9.38). The third and final set of loops is made around the second group but inside those that were made initially – see fig. 9.39.

If you plan to use a ball or weight of some sort inside the knot, place it there at this stage and, with the assistance of a marlin-spike, work the turns of the knot until all the slack is taken out. The job can be finished off by splicing the end into the standing part with an eye splice, as in fig. 9.40, or by seizing it to the standing part if plaited line has been used.

This method produces a three-part monkey's fist, but if this is not big enough or heavy enough (when no weight is used inside), it can be formed with four or five parts. More can be used, but it then becomes very tricky to form.

Fig. 9.41 Heaving-line bend

Fig. 9.42 Choking the luff (1)

Fig. 9.40 Monkey's fist – completion

Fig. 9.43 Choking the luff (2)

Fig. 9.44 Choking the luff (3)

Fig. 9.45 Choking the luff (4)

Heaving-line bend

As the main purpose of a heaving line is to act as a messenger for passing a heavy mooring warp, it is necessary to bend the heaving line to the warp, and the knot usually used is the heaving-line bend.

Quite simply, a bight is formed in the end of the mooring warp and the heaving line is passed through it and racked back and forth across its two parts. The turns are then worked up tight and finished off with a half hitch as shown in fig. 9.41.

Choking the luff

This gruesome sounding exercise is no more than jamming the fall of a tackle, while under load, to prevent it running out. The obvious example of its use is on a mainsail tack downhaul.

First, everything is hove taut and the fall of the tackle is passed inside the other part (or parts) of the tackle to jam across the swallow of the block (fig. 9.42). For added security a half hitch, usually made 'on the bight', is added above the block (fig. 9.43), and out-and-out pessimists go for a second as well (fig. 9.44).

A variation less likely to jam immovably is that shown in fig. 9.45, where the fall has been half hitched around the tackle below the block without the initial jamming across the swallow. This method is not quite so effective as some slack is inevitable.

10 Choosing ropes

Synthetic fibre ropes have many properties that set them above their predecessors of natural fibre such as hemp, sisal, coir or cotton. Synthetics are damp-proof; they have immense strength; they have great resistance to weathering and attack by chemicals; some of them have great elasticity while others have extremely low stretch characteristics; some synthetics are buoyant.

There are three main types of synthetic fibres used for rope-making; nylon, polyester (which most people recognize under the trade names of Terylene, Dacron or Tergal) and polypropylene. In addition to these, a few ropes incorporate Kevlar carbon fibres to give them very high strength and very low stretch properties.

Nylon is far and away the strongest of the synthetics (excluding Kevlar reinforced ones), with tremendous 'give', making it ideal for mooring and anchor warps where it can absorb shock loads. However, this elasticity makes it unsuitable for such things as sheets and halyards, where you would be for ever taking up the slack as it stretched.

Polyester is not quite as strong as nylon, but is still very strong indeed. It has very much lower stretch characteristics than nylon, making it suitable for use as sheets and halyards when used in its 'pre-stretched' form. Pre-stretching is a process that further reduces the elasticity of the rope and helps it to maintain a constant

length. Despite this many people choose to use wire rope for halyards, with a synthetic rope tail spliced on for easy handling, and others go for a Kevlar rope halyard which, although it has to be of larger diameter than wire, is about half the weight and stretches only fractionally more – in other words negligibly.

Polypropylene is somewhat weaker than either nylon or polyester, and is rather susceptible to chafe and abrasion. It does have the advantage of being light and buoyant, making it a very good rope to choose for things like heaving lines. Care should be taken if tempted to buy a cheap un-branded polypropylene rope. Make sure that it contains the necessary inhibitors to protect it from attack and deterioration by ultra-violet radiation (sunlight). Reputable brands (and certainly those conforming to British or American trade standards) will include these inhibitors.

Polypropylene is resistant to attack by most acids and alkalis, while nylon is resistant to alkaline attack but not acid, and polyester is resistant to acid. However, all synthetic rope will suffer if brought into contact with paint solvents.

Synthetic fibres are often made into three-strand hawser-laid ropes, in exactly the same form as natural fibres were, but with synthetics we also have other unique forms, such as plaited sheaths containing plaited, laid or parallel filament cores. Perhaps most significant is the strength produced by having continuous filaments running the full length of the rope, unlike natural fibre ropes, where the fibres are strictly limited in length. Non-continuous (staple) filament ropes are still produced, and when these are used they are stronger, but otherwise almost indistinguishable from cotton rope.

When considering what rope to use for what job the basic questions to ask are: Do you want elasticity or not? Will the rope be twisted frequently? Does the rope need to float?

If stretch is required then you need nylon. For such purposes as anchor warps, a three-strand rope of large diameter (so that it can be held and hauled on easily) may be chosen, or even better a cable-plaited rope (eight-strand plait) such as Marlow's Multiplait which is easily handled, will not mind being twisted by the meanderings of the boat on the turn of each tide, and is easily spliced to the length of chain between the anchor and the warp. A smoother core and sheath nylon warp, such as Marina Super Braidline, may be used, but this is not so easy to hold when wet as the cable-plaited rope, and the rope to chain splice is rather bulky for passing through fairleads or navel pipes.

For such uses as mooring warps, nylon is again first choice for its ability to absorb shock loads. If economics are considered, then a polypropylene rope will suffice, provided that it is well guarded against chafe.

For sheets, there is really no doubt that a braided core and sheath type of polyester rope, such as Braidline, Gemini (Samson) or Cup Sheet is the answer. It is easy on the hands, has low stretch characteristics and is very strong. A lesser alternative, but one perfectly suitable for smaller craft, is a simple plaited rope, rather than a core and sheath type.

Halyards, too, can well be made of a core and sheath rope, though many people favour a wire halyard with a rope fall spliced onto it for easy handling. Cup Sheet, which has very low stretch properties, can be fitted with a special terminal incorporating a halyard snapshackle, without the need for any sort of eyesplice. As an alternative to wire for halyards, Gleistein of Germany produces a Kevlar halyard which is about half the weight of wire and can have its outer sheath stripped off to about the same point as there would otherwise be a rope to wire splice, thus reducing weight and windage aloft while retaining the softer and bulkier fall for handling. For equivalent strength, the Kevlar halyard must be a little larger in diameter than wire, and it needs care when cleating not to cripple the Kevlar filaments. Sheaves must be at least eight times the diameter of the Kevlar core, as opposed to twelve diameters for wire and four for rope. A straightforward three-strand rope can also be used for halyards with complete success, but it is less comfortable to handle than the core and sheath ropes.

With log lines, where the rope is constantly being twisted, a plaited rope is definitely the one to choose, and preferably polyester at that.

The buoyant properties of polypropylene make it the clear choice for heaving lines, and most people prefer to use it in its plaited form. Multifilament polypropylene is also a good choice as it is soft and pliable.

Many plaited ropes are available in a variety of colours – blue, red, green, gold, black – as well as the normal white. This makes it possible to colour code sail handling systems and where several lines are led aft to the cockpit (for instance) this does make life much simpler.

It is hard to say what size of rope to use for a particular job, since for the most part it is a question of what can best be handled. Strength (above a certain diameter) becomes irrelevant as the rope will be more than strong enough for the job. To give examples, a 6 millimetre ($\frac{1}{4}$ inch) diameter nylon Braidline can hold a load roughly equivelent to the weight of a sports car, while one of 10 millimetres ($\frac{13}{32}$ inch) diameter can cope with the weight of a Rolls Royce. When you think that a 10 millimetre ($\frac{13}{32}$ inch) rope is used for mainsheets on boats ranging in size from cruisers of about thirty feet down to small dinghies, you can see that while the bigger boats must

check that the rope is strong enough, the dinghy owner must be choosing simply for ease of handling: strength is no longer the main consideration.

Nevertheless some sort of guide is required, and we can do no better than to quote from the Marina Manual produced by Bridon Fibres and Plastics, makers of Braidline ropes, who themselves base their recommendations on size of rope (Tables 1–5).

Table 1   Halyards (polyester Braidline or pre-stretched polyester three-strand)

Boat length overall (m)	(ft)	Mainsail diameter (mm)	(ins)	Jib diameter (mm)	(ins)	Spinnaker diameter (mm)	(ins)
5	16	6	$\frac{1}{4}$	6	$\frac{1}{4}$	6	$\frac{1}{4}$
7	23	8	$\frac{5}{16}$	8	$\frac{5}{16}$	8	$\frac{5}{16}$
10	33	10	$\frac{13}{32}$	10	$\frac{13}{32}$	8	$\frac{5}{16}$
12	39	12	$\frac{1}{2}$	12	$\frac{1}{2}$	10	$\frac{13}{32}$
15	49	12	$\frac{1}{2}$	12	$\frac{1}{2}$	12	$\frac{1}{2}$
(and over)							

Table 2   Sheets (polyester Braidline or dinghy sheet for smaller sizes)

Boat length overall (m)	(ft)	Main or jib diameter (mm)	(ins)	Genoa diameter (mm)	(ins)	Spinnaker diameter (mm)	(ins)
5	16	10	$\frac{13}{32}$	10	$\frac{13}{32}$	8	$\frac{5}{16}$
7	23	10	$\frac{13}{32}$	10	$\frac{13}{32}$	10	$\frac{13}{32}$
10	33	10	$\frac{13}{32}$	12	$\frac{1}{2}$	12	$\frac{1}{2}$
12	39	12	$\frac{1}{2}$	14	$\frac{9}{16}$	14	$\frac{9}{16}$
15	49	12	$\frac{1}{2}$	16	$\frac{5}{8}$	16	$\frac{5}{8}$

Table 3   Anchor (nylon Braidline or eight-strand plaited)

Boat length overall (m)	(ft)	Nylon diameter (mm)	(ins)
5	16	12	$\frac{1}{2}$
7	23	12	$\frac{1}{2}$
10	33	16	$\frac{5}{8}$
12	39	18	$\frac{3}{4}$
15	49	20	$\frac{13}{16}$

Table 4 *Mooring (staple polypropylene or three-strand nylon)*

Boat length overall (m)	(ft)	Nylon diameter (mm)	(ins)	Polypropylene diameter (mm)	(ins)
5	16	8	$\frac{5}{16}$	10	$\frac{13}{32}$
7	23	12	$\frac{1}{2}$	14	$\frac{9}{16}$
10	33	14	$\frac{9}{16}$	16	$\frac{5}{8}$
12	39	16	$\frac{5}{8}$	20	$\frac{13}{16}$
15	49	18	$\frac{3}{4}$	22	$\frac{7}{8}$

Table 5 *Percentage retained strength of knotted ropes*

Material	Nylon rope A	B	Terylene rope A	B	Fibrefilm polypropylene A	B	Staple polypropylene rope A	B	Sisal rope A	B
Reef knot	50	37	67	45	45	44	65	43	76	53
Overhand knot	54	40	64	43	58	47	59	39	71	50
Bowline	78	58	85	56	58	57	98	64	90	63
Sheet bend	71	53	74	49	62	49	62	41	72	50
Double sheet bend	77	57	63	42	67	54*	69	45	71	50
Clove hitch	74	55	78	52	66	65	78	51	100	81
Eye splice	100	81	100	89	87	86	100	86	100	100
Timber hitch	75	55	98	65	77	61*	86	57	99	94

Note. These results have been established from numerous tests on new ropes in the size range 4–6 mm diameter. Some reduction in these values may be expected from ropes larger in diameter or in a worn condition, and this information should be regarded as advisory only.

All tests except fibrefilm were undertaken on 6 mm ($\frac{1}{4}$ in) diameter rope. Fibrefilm tests (except those marked *) were performed on 14 mm diameter rope.

The two columns relate to calculations based on the rated breaking strengths of the ropes (column A) and on the actual breaking strengths of the ropes (column B), as follows:

$$\text{Column A} \quad \frac{\text{average knot breaking strength}}{\text{rated breaking strength of rope}} \times 100$$

$$\text{Column B} \quad \frac{\text{average knot breaking strength}}{\text{actual breaking strength of rope}} \times 100$$

100

11　Fancy work

Since decorative ropework is a subject for a book in its own right, we are only mentioning a few simple ideas here to encourage the reader to make further studies. Making different types of fancy work is an absorbing pastime, and much of it is useful stuff.

The best material for work of this sort is probably a small-diameter, solid, plaited polyester cord (unless a laid line is particularly needed). Don't try to work with a hollow cord as this will not retain its shape nicely when the knots are worked tight.

Turk's head

The turk's head is probably the most widely known and used of all fancy knots, being simple to tie and yet having an almost infinite variety of forms and uses. The one described here is just about the simplest form of the knot.

The cord is first laid around the object over which the knot is to be tied, as though about to make a clove hitch (fig. 11.1), but instead of tucking the working end parallel to the lazy end, it is passed across the standing part and tucked under (fig. 11.2). The two standing parts beyond it are crossed over each other (fig. 11.3), the upper down over the lower. The working end is then passed downwards under the new upper part as in fig. 11.4. The parts are crossed

Fig. 11.1 Turk's head – forming (1)

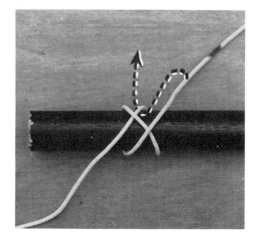

Fig. 11.2 Turk's head – forming (2)

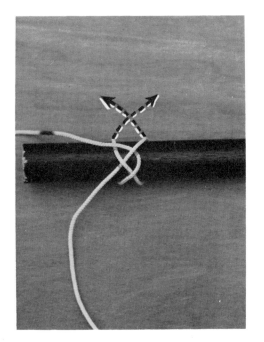

Fig. 11.3 Turk's head – forming (3)

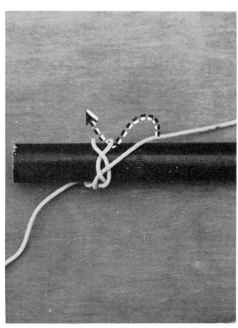

Fig. 11.5 Turk's head – forming (5)

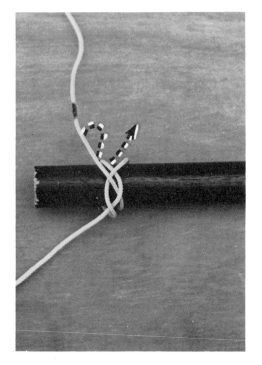

Fig. 11.4 Turk's head – forming (4)

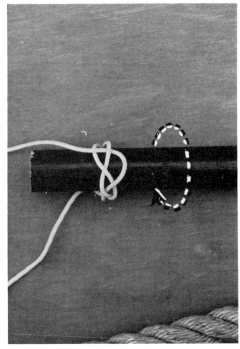

Fig. 11.6 Turk's head – forming (6)

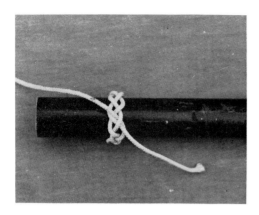

Fig. 11.7 Turk's head – forming (7)

again, this time bottom over top, and the working end is passed upwards under the new lower part as in fig. 11.5. The work is then turned round (fig. 11.6) and the lazy end is passed down parallel to the working end to produce a situation as in fig. 11.7. This completes the first round and the knot may now be doubled once or twice. The turk's head shown in fig. 11.8 has been doubled twice by following round the whole knot twice each time paralleling the leads already there. Finally the knot is worked up tight and the ends are cut off so that they are hidden under a crossing point.

The turk's head may be used decoratively, as in fig. 11.9, where two have been put on a launch's whipstaff tiller, or it can be used practically as in the examples shown in figs 11.10 and 11.11. In the first it is being used on a halyard to stop the serving on the eye splice jamming in the swallow of a masthead block, and in the second it has been formed in large-diameter rope round a spar to act as a fender against a dinghy slung in davits.

Grommet

The grommet is essentially a practical piece of work, but as it is neither knot, bend, nor hitch, it really has to come under fancy work. Grommets are often used to reinforce lacing holes and may also be used as slings. They used to be in common use for stropping wooden blocks, but nowadays such blocks are rarities.

A strand is unlaid from a three-strand rope and is formed into a circle as in fig. 11.12. The ends are then laid spirally round in a right-handed manner if the strand came from a right-handed rope, and left-handed from a left-handed rope. One end is laid round (fig. 11.13) then the other fills in. Finally, the ends are tucked against the lay (fig. 11.14) to produce a completed grommet.

Half-hitching

This is a simple but attractive way of covering a rope, spar, or bottle and in each case provides a non-slip grip. A simple series of half hitches is formed, each one looping on to the next and being formed around the loop between two half hitches in the row above. The pattern is clearly shown in fig. 11.15. When worked in small stuff it is generally done with a needle-and-palm, but it can also be made in larger rope as a covering for a fender.

Fender hitching

Another form of half-hitching is fender hitching, the difference being that whereas the half hitches described above were made around loops, in fender hitching they are made around the hitches themselves in the row above. Again, fig. 11.16 makes the process quite clear.

As the name implies, fender hitching is often used to cover fenders, but may also be used to decorate bottles. If the hitches are kept well together the result is very like ribbed knitting.

103

Fig. 11.8 Turk's head – completion

Fig. 11.10 Turk's head – practical use (1)

Fig. 11.9 Turk's head – decorative use

Fig. 11.11 Turk's head – practical use (2)

Fig. 11.12 Grommet – forming (1)   Fig. 11.13 Grommet – forming (2)   Fig. 11.14 Grommet – completion

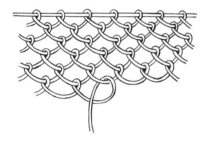

Fig. 11.15 Half hitching

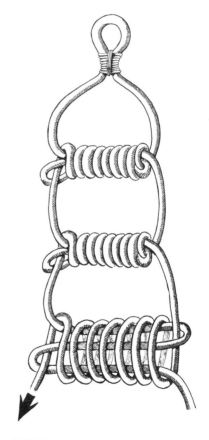

Fig. 11.16 Fender hitching

Fig. 11.17 Rope ladder

Fig. 11.18 Coachwhipping – forming (1)

Fig. 11.19 Coachwhipping – forming (2)

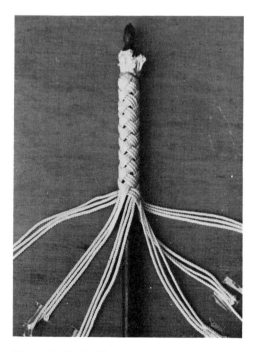

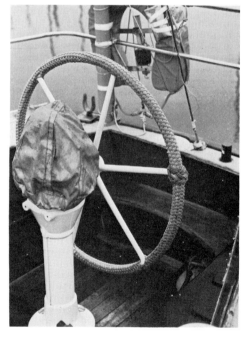

Fig. 11.20 Coachwhipping – forming (3)

Fig. 11.21 Coachwhipping completion

Rope ladder

Boarding ladders are particularly useful on boats with high freeboard. They make climbing aboard from a tender much easier and particularly aid the recovery of anyone from the water. However, they are not cheap to buy when made of stainless steel and teak, or even light alloy and knotty pine. Much more practical is this rope ladder which stows easily, and whose construction can be followed from fig. 11.17. Using rope of about 12–14 millimetre ($\frac{1}{2}$-inch) diameter you'll need roughly six fathoms for a two metre length of ladder.

Fig. 11.22 Alternate crown sennit

Coachwhipping

Coachwhipping is often used to cover stanchions or rails or even the mast thrust pillar in the cabin of a boat with deck-stepped mast. It is worked with an even number of strands seized at one end of the rail and distributed evenly around its circumference. The strands are then split into groups and interwoven about the rail in the fashion shown in figs 11.18 and 11.19. In these diagrams single strands have been used for clarity, but the method is also shown using six groups of three strands each in fig. 11.20, and a finished whipping is shown on the wheel in fig. 11.21. On a stanchion or rail, both sets of ends would have something like a turk's head put on to hide the end seizings.

Fig. 11.23 Alternate crown sennit four-strand pattern

Alternate crown sennit

This is an attractive piece for key fobs or short lanyards attached to the pins of snap shackles (fig. 11.22) to facilitate their opening.

A pair of cords are centred through the ring (of the key or shackle pin) and one is laid across to the left in front of the part on the left. That strand is laid over the first and

in front of the one on its left. The third strand is laid over that and in front of the one on its left, the fourth strand. This one is laid over the third and tucked through the bight formed in the first-laid strand. This pattern is shown in fig. 11.23 and is actually a series of crown knots (page 108) made with four strands instead of three. Now the same over-and-under pattern is worked again, only this time to the right. After that it is worked back again to the left, and so on as far as you like. To finish, the ends may be worked back into the sennit.

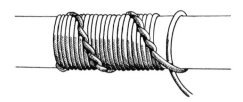

Fig. 11.24 French whipping

Fig. 11.25 French whipping – covered ends

This method of alternate crowning produces a roughly square sennit. If the crowns are always made in one direction (instead of alternately left and right as described above), the result will be a spiral.

French whipping

This is another decorative covering for stanchions, rails and the like, based simply on half hitches. A line is first anchored to the object being covered with a clove hitch, one of whose ends is used to form a continuous series of half hitches around the object as in fig. 11.24. The pattern can be followed for as many revolutions as you like, i.e. until the required length is achieved.

Usually, the ends are covered with some form of turk's head as can be seen on the tiller covering in fig. 11.25.

Square sennit

The square sennit, not so many years ago, was used as packing for engine parts, but it stands on its own as a decorative piece of fancy work, or it can be used to cover a spar of some sort, or make a dog lead.

Generally, the square sennit is made with eight strands, in which case they are seized together at their ends and divided into two groups of four, one on the right and one on the left. The outer strand from the right-hand side is passed around the back and for-

ward between the middle pair on the left side (so that there are two strands on its left and two on its right) as in fig. 11.26, and led back to the group on the right-hand side. Then the outer strand on the left-hand side is led round the back and passed forward between the middle pair on the right-hand side (as in fig. 11.27) and taken across to join its original group on the left-hand side. This process is repeated taking strands from, alternately, the left- and right-hand groups. The pattern soon emerges and can be seen in fig. 11.28.

Crown knot

The crown knot is never used alone as it would easily come undone, but it forms the basis of several stopper knots or knob knots, including the manrope knot (page 109). Begin by unlaying the rope and interweaving the strands as in fig. 11.29, being careful to follow the direction of the rope's lay. Then work them tight as shown in fig. 11.30 to finish.

Wall knot

The wall knot is simply a crown knot (above) made upside down. Each strand is passed around the next in the same direction as the rope's lay, and then up through the bights to emerge at the top in the pat-

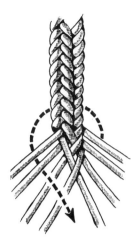

Fig. 11.26 Square sennit – forming (1)

Fig. 11.27 Square sennit – forming (2)

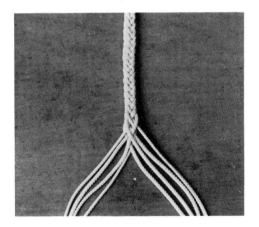

Fig. 11.28 Square sennit – completion

Fig. 11.29 Crown knot – forming

tern shown in fig. 11.31. The knot is worked tight to look like that in fig. 11.32. If the wall knot is then doubled, that is to say each part of the knot is followed through again, you end up with the useful end knot known (logically) as the double wall knot shown in fig. 11.33.

Manrope knot

Start by making a wall knot (page 108) and then with the three strands that emerge make a crown knot (page 108) on top. Leave

Fig. 11.30 Crown knot – completion

Fig. 11.31 Wall knot – forming (1)

Fig. 11.32 Wall knot – forming (2)

Fig. 11.34 Manrope knot – forming

Fig. 11.33 Wall knot – completion

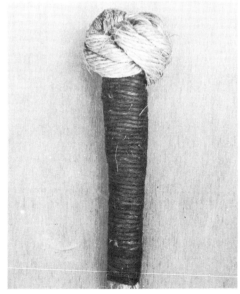

Fig. 11.35 Manrope knot – completion

110

Fig. 11.36 Matthew Walker knot – forming (1)

Fig. 11.39 Matthew Walker knot – completion

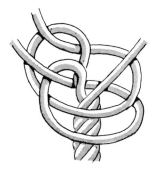

Fig. 11.37 Matthew Walker knot – forming (2)

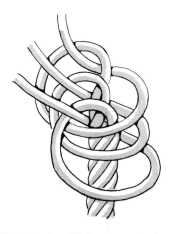

Fig. 11.38 Matthew Walker knot – forming (3)

all parts of the knots loose and open and follow each part of the wall knot around with the corresponding strands until every part has been doubled. Now double the crown

knot on top. Next pass each strand down through the centre of the knot until they protrude at the bottom (fig. 11.34) and work the knot tight with a fid or marlinspike. The ends may now either be cut off, spliced into the lay, or tapered and covered with marling as in fig. 11.35.

To remember the sequence of events remember the rhyme:

First a wall,
And then a crown,
Next tuck up,
And then tuck down.

Matthew Walker knot

One of the best and most attractive of all stopper knots, it is formed by passing each strand around the rope in the direction of the lay and tucking it upward through its own bight, as in fig. 11.36. Follow the sequence carefully through figs 11.37 and 11.38, then work the knot up tight. To finish off lay up the strands and whip them with a needle-and-palm whipping as shown in fig. 11.39.

12 Tips

Hoisting furled flags

When hoisting say a Q flag on entry to a foreign port, try folding it in half (along the hoist), rolling it (from the fly towards the hoist), and securing it as shown in fig. 12.1. When hoisted, the fall of the halyard is jerked and the flag breaks out, whereupon the halyard is set up and cleated. In this way the flag is hoisted clear and is not likely to snag in the rigging as it might otherwise do. One point to remember: it is a matter of etiquette that ensigns are *never* hoisted in this way.

Highwayman's cutaway

This is a slippery hitch that will hold a load applied to the left-hand end. Follow the figures through from 12.2 to 12.5, keeping the load on the left-hand end. To undo the hitch just pull on the right-hand (slipped) end. This hitch is useful for towing or when carrying a kedge over the stern of a dinghy as it is being laid out.

Portuguese bowline

This is sometimes also referred to as the French bowline and is very good as an emergency bosun's chair, since a man may sit in one loop and have the other around his back for support.

Fig. 12.1 Hoisting furled flag

An overhand loop is formed in the standing part, the working end is passed forward through it twice to make large bights as in fig. 12.6. The end is passed round the standing part and back downward through the first-formed overhand loop (fig. 12.7). The knot is then worked tight and the bights adjusted to the required lengths.

Lashing sheerlegs

When setting up sheerlegs, for instance to lift out an engine, the heads of the spars are lashed together starting with a timber hitch

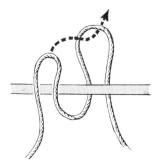

Fig. 12.2 Highwayman's cutaway (1)

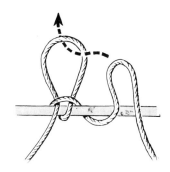

Fig. 12.4 Highwayman's cutaway (3)

Fig. 12.3 Highwayman's cutaway (2)

Fig. 12.5 Highwayman's cutaway (4)

Fig. 12.6 Portuguese bowline (1)

Fig. 12.7 Portuguese bowline (2)

Fig. 12.8 Lashing sheerlegs (1)

Fig. 12.9 Lashing sheerlegs (2)

(page 18) around one leg followed by a number of tightly laid-on round turns over both. The end is then passed forward between the spars, up across the turns and taken behind one spar and forward between the heads (fig. 12.8). This end is taken diagonally down across the turns, back round the other spar, and forward again between the two spars. The figure-of-eight pattern so formed is then repeated several times and finished off with some half hitches around one head (fig. 12.9). These turns tighten as the legs of the rig are splayed apart, and this really is the essence of the lashing – it is put on with the spars laid together, and then tightened by placing them apart.

Old rope stops

Don't throw old lengths of rope away but cut them into short lengths (about 3 feet) and use the rope yarns as seizing material. Figure 12.10 shows how the yarns are pulled out, one at a time when needed. A common use for them is when making up a heavy, large-diameter rope for stowage. Keep the yarns double, pass them around the coil, and form a cow hitch (page 13) by passing the ends through the bight (fig. 12.11). Finish off with a slipped half hitch

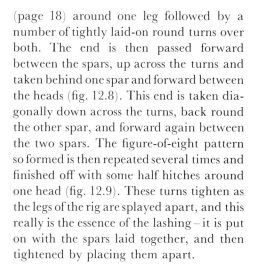

for quick release (fig. 12.12). The coil is generally stopped off with three such seizings.

Dipping eyes on bollards

When making fast to a bollard that already has one or more other mooring lines made up on it, dip the eye of your own warp under the existing ones (fig. 12.13), and drop it down over the top (fig. 12.14). If this is done then you and the other boats can slip independently; otherwise the other chap will not be able to let go his line without letting go yours as well – and he just might not resecure it properly – or he'll take delight in dragging you out of your bunk in the middle of a cold wet night.

Cleating wire falls

The 'dog's dinner' in fig. 12.15 is not quite as bad as it appears, but it does show what a nuisance wire falls can be when there is more than will fit on a winch drum. The answer, as shown here, is to pass a number of turns around the drum and cleat before turning up the rope tail in the normal fashion (page 82) and finishing with a half-

114

Fig. 12.10 Old rope stops (1)

Fig. 12.12 Old rope stops (3)

Fig. 12.11 Old rope stops (2)

Fig. 12.14 (*right*) Dipping eyes on bollards (2)

Fig. 12.13 Dipping eyes on bollards (1)

Fig. 12.15 Cleating wire falls

hitch coil (page 74). This method of dealing with the wire, rather than turning it up on the cleat, saves it being crippled by the tight turns cleating would entail.

Frapping turns for tightness

When preparing for sea, absolutely everything that could move must be lashed down tightly, and that includes dinghies or spare fuel drums. Where such things are regularly carried on deck, shaped chocks and eyebolts should be installed to make lashing easier. If this is done then turns are put over the dinghy or drums and are pulled tightly together with horizontal frapping turns as shown in fig. 12.16. The end is finished off with half hitches round these turns. The frapping turns should be hove really taut to ensure a secure lashing.

Bowline bend

This is a very simple, very secure way of joining any two lines together. If we are perfectly honest it is the bend that most of us use when we can't remember what the 'correct' bend is! As can be seen from fig. 12.17 the bowline bend consists of two interlocking bowlines – it really could not be much more straightforward.

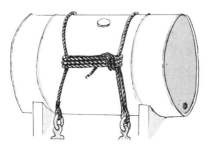

Fig. 12.16 Frapping turns for tightness

Fig. 12.17 Bowline bend

Fig. 12.18 Bowsing down (1)

Fig. 12.19 Bowsing down (2)

Fig. 12.20 Bowsing down (3)

Fig. 12.21 Bowsing down (4)

Fig. 12.22 Bowsing down (5)

Bowsing down

Bowsing down means heaving down taut on a lashing which (for example) is securing a dinghy on deck. To get a really good purchase on such a lashing the waggoner's hitch (page 17) is often used, but the following system works just as well. A line rising from an eyebolt on deck is passed in a loop through an eye in the lashing (fig. 12.18). The end is then passed back down through the eyebolt (fig. 12.19) and brought up through the loop that was first formed (fig. 12.20). Now by hauling down on this end a 2 : 1 purchase is achieved and the lashing can be bowsed down hard. Once this has been done it is secured by taking the end through the eyebolt and half hitching it round all the standing parts (fig. 12.21), finishing with a tuck between the standing parts (fig. 12.22).

117

Fig. 12.23 Double overhand knot – first shape

Fig. 12.25 Double figure-of-eight

Fig. 12.24 Double overhand knots – second shape

Double overhand knot

This is an overhand knot with an extra tuck, as used at the start of the surgeon's knot (page 14), formed in the end of a line to stop it passing through an eye. It has the advantage over a single overhand knot of being bulkier, but it does tend to jam more tightly than say a double figure-of-eight (below). The double overhand knot can be worked into either of the two shapes shown in figs 12.23 and 12.24, the one in fig. 12.23 being occasionally used as the basis of a decorative knot.

Double figure-of-eight

The double figure-of-eight is used when a single one is of insufficient size to guarantee stopping the end of, say, a halyard from running out through an eye or block. As can be seen in fig. 12.25 it is formed in the same way as an ordinary figure-of-eight, but with an extra turn taken round the standing part before tucking the end down through the first loop. It is generally considered a more seamanlike knot than the double overhand knot described on page 118, in part because it does not jam so readily.

Netting

Netting stretched along the guardrails either side of the foredeck helps to prevent either lowered sails or small children from going overboard. It is simple to make, consisting as it does of a series of sheet bends. The diagram (fig. 12.26) shows how to

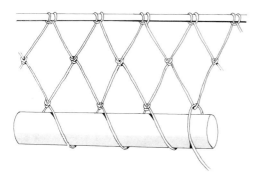

Fig. 12.26 Netting: general arrangement. Note use of spacer (bottom)

begin with a row of clove hitches on a rail and the use of a suitable size spacer to keep the openings in the netting even. Figure 12.27 shows how the sheet bend is formed

Fig. 12.27 Netting; sheet bend

on the bight of each loop. A shuttle or netting needle (obtainable from fishermen's supply stores) is used to carry the netting twine.

The Hunter's Bend

This is claimed to be a new knot, but some suggest it has been in use for the greater part of a century in the airship service. In this role it was known as the Zeppelin bend. The great strength of this bend, which is used for joining two ropes together, is that it holds securely with some of the cheaper modern ropes, such as Courlene and Ulstron, which have hard and slippery surfaces. Certainly it is superior to the sheet bend. See figs. 12.28–12.31.

Fig. 12.28 Hunter's Bend (1)

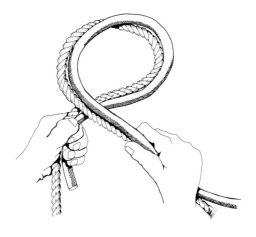

Fig. 12.29 Hunter's Bend (2)

Fig. 12.30 Hunter's Bend (3)

Fig. 12.31 Hunter's Bend (4)

Acknowledgements

We are grateful to Bridon Fibres and Plastics Ltd for permission to reproduce tables 1–5 in chapter 10.

Some of our photographs and drawings have previously appeared in articles in *Yachting Monthly*, *Practical Boat Owner* (UK), *Sail* (USA), *Yachts and Yachting* (UK), and *Cruising World* (USA).

Index